Also by C. K. Williams

POETRY

A Day for Anne Frank · *Lies* · *I Am the Bitter Name* ·
The Lark. The Thrush. The Starling. (Poems from Issa) ·
With Ignorance · *Tar* · *Flesh and Blood* · *Poems, 1963–1983* ·
Helen · *A Dream of Mind* · *Selected Poems* ·
The Vigil · *Repair* · *Love About Love* · *The Singing* · *Collected
Poems* · *Creatures* · *Wait* · *Writers Writing Dying* · *Catherine's
Laughter* · *All at Once* · *Selected Later Poems* · *Falling Ill*

ESSAYS

Poetry and Consciousness · *On Whitman* · *In Time: Poets, Poems,
and the Rest*

MEMOIR

Misgivings: My Mother, My Father, Myself

TRANSLATIONS

Sophocles' *Women of Trachis* (with Gregory W. Dickerson) · *The Bacchae
of Euripides* · *Canvas*, by Adam Zagajewski (with Renata Gorczynski
and Benjamin Ivry) · *Francis Ponge: Selected Poems* (with
John Montague and Margaret Guiton)

CHILDREN'S BOOKS

How the Nobble Was Finally Found · *A Not Scary Story About
Big Scary Things*

INVISIBLE MENDING

INVISIBLE MENDING

The Best of C. K. Williams

C. K. Williams

Introduction by Alan Shapiro

Farrar, Straus and Giroux
New York

Farrar, Straus and Giroux
120 Broadway, New York 10271

Printed in the United States of America
First edition, 2024

Library of Congress Cataloging-in-Publication Data
Names: Williams, C. K. (Charles Kenneth), 1936–2015 author. | Shapiro, Alan,
    1952– author of introduction.
Title: Invisible mending : the best of C. K. Williams / C. K., Williams ;
    introduction by Alan Shapiro.
Description: First edition. | New York : Farrar, Straus and Giroux, 2024. |
    Includes index.
Identifiers: LCCN 2023040977 | ISBN 9780374608392 (paperback)
Subjects: LCGFT: Poetry.
Classification: LCC PS3573.I4483 I58 2024 | DDC 811/.54—dc23/eng/20231003
LC record available at https://lccn.loc.gov/2023040977

Designed by Patrice Sheridan

Our books may be purchased in bulk for promotional, educational, or business
use. Please contact your local bookseller or the Macmillan Corporate and
Premium Sales Department at 1-800-221-7945, extension 5442, or by email at
MacmillanSpecialMarkets@macmillan.com.

www.fsgbooks.com
Follow us on social media at @fsgbooks

10 9 8 7 6 5 4 3 2 1

Contents

Introduction: Hedgehog and Fox, by Alan Shapiro ✦ *xi*

from *Lies* (1969)
A Day for Anne Frank ✦ 3
Being Alone ✦ 9

from *I Am the Bitter Name* (1972)
Yours ✦ 13

from *With Ignorance* (1977)
Bread ✦ 17
Spit ✦ 20
The Shade ✦ 23
With Ignorance ✦ 25
Near the Haunted Castle ✦ 34
Hog Heaven ✦ 36

from *Tar* (1983)
Combat ✦ 41
Tar ✦ 50

From My Window ✦ 53

My Mother's Lips ✦ 56

On Learning of a Friend's Illness ✦ 58

Waking Jed ✦ 61

The Gas Station ✦ 64

from *Flesh and Blood* (1987)

Hooks ✦ 69

Peace ✦ 70

The Lens ✦ 71

Dawn ✦ 72

Reading: Winter ✦ 73

Reading: The Gym ✦ 74

Vehicle: Forgetting ✦ 75

Alzheimer's: The Wife ✦ 76

Alzheimer's: The Husband ✦ 77

Even So ✦ 78

The Prodigy ✦ 79

The City in the Hills ✦ 80

Rush Hour ✦ 81

The Storm ✦ 82

Love: Beginnings ✦ 83

from Le Petit Salvié ✦ 84

First Desires ✦ 85

from *A Dream of Mind* (1992)

The Silence ✦ 89

Politics ✦ 91

When ✦ 93

A Dream of Mind

The Method ✦ 97

Shadows ✦ 99

Vocations • 101

The Solid • 103

The Charge • 105

The Crime • 107

Shells • 109

Room • 111

History • 113

The Gap • 115

The Knot • 117

The Fear • 119

You • 120

To Listen • 121

The Covenant • 123

Light • 125

from *The Vigil* (1997)

My Fly • 129

Instinct • 131

Garden (Symbols) • 132

Realms • 133

The Bed • 135

Grace • 137

Exterior: Day • 139

Time: 1972 • 140

Time: 1978 • 141

The Lover • 143

from *Repair* (1999)

Ice • 147

After Auschwitz • 149

The Dress • 152

The Train • 156

Depths • 157

Tree • 159

The Dance • 160

Swifts • 161

Owen: Seven Days • 162

Invisible Mending • 165

from *The Singing* (2003)

The Doe • 169

The Singing • 170

Sully: Sixteen Months • 172

Of Childhood the Dark • 174

The World • 182

from *Wait* (2010)

The Gaffe • 185

Marina • 188

Cassandra, Iraq • 190

Wait • 192

The Coffin Store • 193

Thrush • 195

We • 197

All but Always • 199

Back • 201

The Foundation • 202

Jew on Bridge • 204

from *Writers Writing Dying* (2012)

The Day Continues Lovely • 211

from *All at Once* (2014)

The Last Circus • 217

Again • 218

Silence ✦ 219

The Broom ✦ 220

from *Catherine's Laughter*

Talk ✦ 223

Oaks ✦ 224

from *Selected Later Poems* (2015)

The World and Hokusai ✦ 227

Beethoven Invents the Species Again ✦ 229

from *Falling III* (2017)

Box ✦ 233

First Dying ✦ 234

You ✦ 235

Eyes ✦ 236

Secrets ✦ 237

Impatience ✦ 238

Friends ✦ 239

Embrace ✦ 240

Lonely ✦ 241

Air ✦ 242

Index of Titles and First Lines ✦ 243

Introduction:
Hedgehog and Fox

by Alan Shapiro

In a famous essay on Tolstoy, Isaiah Berlin divides writers and thinkers into two opposing camps, two kinds of animals, hedgehogs and foxes: hedgehogs, who "relate everything to a single central vision, one system, less or more coherent or articulate, in terms of which they understand, think and feel—a single, universal, organising principle in terms of which alone is all that they are and say has significance;" and foxes, who "pursue many ends . . . moving on many levels, seizing upon the essence of a vast variety of experiences and objects for what they are in themselves, without, consciously or unconsciously, seeking to fit them into, or exclude them from, any one unchanging, all-embracing . . . unitary inner vision." The hedgehog mind prefers intensity and purity over range and balance; the fox prefers open-ended adaptable modes of thinking and feeling. If the Ur hedgehog in Western literature is Achilles in his great passionate uncompromising outrage and bloodlust, the Ur fox is Odysseus, the man of many ways.

These metaphors of hedgehog and fox provide an illuminating way to think about the dramatic change that C. K. Williams's poetry underwent between his first two books, *Lies* and *I Am the Bitter Name*, and *With Ignorance*. Almost overnight, it seems, Williams goes from being a young, very talented but somewhat typical American poet of the late nineteen sixties/early seventies, to one of the most groundbreaking, consequential poets of his or any generation. He trades in a hedgehog singleness of tone and style for the unpredictably various colorations of a fox. The metamorphosis is marked not only by a turn from short lines to the long line he became famous for, but also and more crucially by a turn from a hyperintense poetry of lyric fragments to a more inclusive poetry that utilizes, without loss of intensity, all the tools of essay writing and prose fiction, a poetry that can explicitly articulate or investigate relationships among things as opposed to listing, juxtaposing, or presenting things implicitly related; a poetry that can think about what it's feeling and feel intensely the consequences of its thought, or evoke a memory or tell a story and at the same time meditate on the nature of memory or storytelling.

Here is how Williams himself describes the turn his work took:

> When I first developed the long line I guess I'm known for, it was because I'd felt too constrained not so much by the length of the lines in the poetry I'd been writing as by the conventions of expression that I'd inherited and learned to use . . . I just felt I was leaving too much of myself out in the poetry I'd been writing; my inner life, my response to the world, was so much more complex than what I'd been honing myself down to fit in poems. I heard my work once characterized as "the act of the mind in meditation," and that for me is a good description of what the poems in longer lines evolved to, what I'd unconsciously felt was feasible for them. Perhaps just as important was the fact that the longer lines revealed cadences of thought and observation that weren't available to me before I began to use them.
>
> FROM *IN TIME*, PAGE 120

In a kind of positive feedback loop, the change of style allows for a change of mind that in turns allows for the discovery of yet new styles and forms. The conventions of his early work, which were the conventions of that moment—fragmented, disjunctive, surreal, grounded in lyric feeling, prizing extreme emotion over social context even if emotion has its roots in social context—simply left out too much experience. Those conventions were exclusive, in other words—allowing some aspects of consciousness free rein while ignoring or suppressing others.

The hunger for inclusiveness, for range as well as depth, horizontality of interest as well as verticality of feeling, is where the fox-like turn in Williams's work is most apparent. It's not that he came to devalue intensity as a literary quality; it's that he came to see that there are other qualities equally important. To paraphrase the art critic Edgar Wind, immediacy is an intrinsic good but if all a poem attempts to do is be immediate, it may in fact produce an opposite effect. The eyes may be the most beautiful feature of the face but that doesn't mean a face would be more beautiful if it were all eyes.

I can best illustrate the depth and extent of the transformation by placing a section from "A Day for Anne Frank," a poem from his first book, *Lies*, next to "Hooks," an eight-line poem from his 1987 volume, *Flesh and Blood*:

They are cutting babies in half on bets.
The beautiful sergeant has enough money to drink
for a week.
The beautiful lieutenant can't stop betting.
The little boy whimpers
he'll be good.
The beautiful cook is gathering up meat
for the dogs.
The beautiful dogs
love it all.
Their flanks glisten.
They curl up in their warm kennels
and breathe.
They breathe.

Hooks

Possibly because she's already so striking—tall, well-dressed, very clear,
   pure skin—
when the girl gets on the subway at Lafayette Street everyone notices her
   artificial hand
but we also manage, as we almost always do, not to be noticed noticing,
   except one sleeping woman,
who hasn't budged since Brooklyn but who lifts her head now, opens up,
   forgets herself,
and frankly stares at those intimidating twists of steel, the homely leather
   sock and laces,
so that the girl, as she comes through the door, has to do in turn now
   what is to be done,
which is to look down at it, too, a bit askance, with an air of tolerant,
   bemused annoyance,
the way someone would glance at their unruly, apparently ferocious but
   really quite friendly dog.

The most obvious difference between these two poems is the syntax. In
the early poem the sentences are all simple, declarative, and end-stopped.
Each line is a separate image, the section itself a stack of images, and the
images are generalized figures of brutality and helplessness, with little or no
particularity. The single eight-line sentence of "Hooks" is hypotactic, full of
qualification and subordination, reflecting or enacting the evolving observa-
tions and perceptions of the speaker as the scene unfolds before him. In "A
Day for Anne Frank," the speaker's point of view is fixed, unchanging; even
Anne Frank, to whom much of the poem is addressed, is less a person in her
own right than a projection of the speaker's anguish and horror. The point
of view in "Hooks," on the other hand, is protean, shape-shifting, migrating
from the speaker, who represents the collective voice/viewpoint of the subway
passengers, noticing the artificial hand while pretending not to, to the half-

asleep woman who wakes up and stares at "those intimidating twists of steel,"
to the young woman herself, who sees the prosthesis as a ferocious looking but
really quite friendly dog. As the viewpoint changes, so too does the language,
the imagery. As representative of the well-mannered commuter, the speaker
notices the artificial hand but doesn't describe it; through the not fully con-
scious staring woman he goes beyond mere naming, to the literal description
of those intimidating twists of steel, the homely sock and laces, and when he
makes the jump from staring woman to bemused girl, he employs a simile (the
only figurative image in the poem) to capture or reflect the girl's inner sense of
what the public sees. And all this in a single complex sentence that empatheti-
cally evokes multiple points of view at a particular moment in a specific place.

Like many of the descriptive-narrative poems Williams is famous for,
"Hooks" makes subtle use of free indirect style, a technique most often seen
in prose fiction, but rarely in poetry of any kind, narrative or otherwise. Free
indirect style is a subspecies of limited third-person narration, in which a
narrating voice is inflected by a character's idiom, collapsing without entirely
closing the distance between self and other. It's an instrument of empathy en-
abling us to hear other people's unspoken thoughts in a language they might
use if they were speaking. We don't just see the young girl look down at her
artificial hand, we hear her bemusement in that "really quite friendly" simile
the speaker extrapolates from her look.

This ability to move swiftly and without transition into and out of dif-
fering points of view is one of the great achievements of C. K. Williams's
mature work, one of the best examples of which is "Instinct," from his 1997
book, *The Vigil*:

Although he's apparently the youngest (his little Rasta-beard is barely
    down and feathers),
most casually connected (he hardly glances at the girl he's with, though
    she might be his wife),
half-sloshed (or more than half) on picnic-whiskey teenaged father, when
    his little son,

two or so, tumbles from the slide, hard enough to scare himself, hard
   enough to make him cry,

really cry, not partly cry, not pretend the fright for what must be some
   scarce attention,

but really let it out, let loudly be revealed the fear of having been so close
   to real fear,

he, the father, knows just how quickly he should pick the child up, then
   how firmly hold it,

fit its head into the muscled socket of his shoulder, rub its back, croon
   and whisper to it,

and finally pull away a little, about a head's length, looking, still con-
   cerned, into its eyes,

then smiling, broadly, brightly, as though something had been shared,
   something of importance,

not dreadful, or not very, not at least now that it's past, but rather
   something . . . funny,

funny, yes, it was funny, wasn't it, to fall and cry like that, though one
   certainly can understand,

we've all had glimpses of a premonition of the anguish out there, you're
   better now, though,

aren't you, why don't you go back and try again, I'll watch you, maybe
   have another drink,

yes, my son, my love, I'll go back and be myself now: you go be the person
   you are, too.

I love how this poem moves from father to son and then back to fa-
ther, and the way the changing pronouns track the changing points of view,
culminating in that imagined second-person fusion of father and poet. The
proliferation of subordinate clauses that qualify perception and then qualify
the qualification, that jump forward or reverse direction, or repeat them-
selves with slight but crucial modifications, enact/embody the speaker's
commitment to getting the scene right, to doing justice to these people, de-

scribing their interactions as carefully as he can, in such a way that brings to light both the invisible bonds they share, and the psychological and social hardships they face.

I don't mean to suggest that the later work is less passionately political than the early poems. Or that Williams turns away from lyricism or emotional intensity in favor of a more measured engagement with the world, or that he only writes poems in long lines after *I Am the Bitter Name*. In the later books, he experiments with different kinds of lines. And early and late, even at intimate moments, he's haunted and enraged by social injustice, environmental depredation, and war. His subject matter (the fragility of human bonds and attachments in a violent world) hardly changes. What does change, though, is his imaginative and tonal range, his ever-developing commitment to modes of expression supple enough to explore political outrage in relation to a wide array of other states of feeling in an equally wide array of circumstances and occasions. In his hands, the long line itself becomes a remarkably flexible instrument, accommodating almost any kind of subject or experience—the formal equivalent of a speaking voice that, as occasion warrants, can cry (as in "Jew on Bridge" from *Wait*) or sing (as in "Swifts" from *Repair*), but whose default mode is the voice of someone companionably speculating, talking, brooding, observing, working through intractable complexities, ever skeptical of the very certainties he can't help longing for.

Which is to say, early and late, Williams is never all hedgehog, or all fox. While I do think a hedgehog consistency of manner (one big stylistic idea) defines and limits his early work, what makes his best work so vital is the way both tendencies persist in varying degrees, pushing and pulling against each other. If the fox-like love of particulars and meditative agility distinguishes his mature imagination and practice, one still feels the continuing presence of or desire for an absolute or systematic understanding of experience. It's a manifestation of the fox-like nature of his best poems that they are never purely fox-like.

No poet of his generation has done as much as Williams to reclaim vast territories of human experience that poetry had abandoned to prose genres and popular culture. If American poetry today is, as I believe it is, more diverse than ever, more open to any and all forms of life, more vitally engaged with a world external to the self and shared with others, it's because of what the poems in this volume accomplished. Whether they know it or not, whether they've even read him or not, C. K. Williams set the table for all poets who now tell stories, or think out loud about the stories they tell, even as they tell them, and who regard the sentence as an expressive resource whose interplay of clauses can dramatize the inextricable interplay of thought and feeling, or individual identity and public history, or the hedgehog's love of one great comprehensive understanding and the fox's passion for a contingent world of irreducible particulars.

From

Lies

(1969)

A Day for Anne Frank

God hates you!

1.

I look onto an alley here
where, though tough weeds and flowers thrust up
through cracks and strain
toward the dulled sunlight,
there is the usual filth spilling from cans,
the heavy soot shifting in the gutters.
People come by mostly
to walk their dogs or take the shortcut
between the roaring main streets,
or just to walk
and stare up at the smoky windows,
but this morning when I looked out
children were there running back and forth
between the houses toward me.
They were playing with turtles—
skimming them down the street
like pennies or flat stones,
and bolting, shouting, after the broken corpses.
One had a harmonica, and as he ran,
his cheeks bloating and collapsing like a heart,
I could hear its bleat, and then the girls' screams
suspended behind them with their hair,
and all of them: their hard, young breath,
their feet pounding wildly on the pavement to the corner.

2.

I thought of you at that age.
Little Sister, I thought of you,
thin as a door,
and of how your thighs would have swelled
and softened like cake,
your breasts have bleached
and the new hair growing on you like song
would have stiffened and gone dark.
There was rain for a while, and then not.
Because no one came, I slept again,
and dreamed that you were here with me,
snarled on me like wire,
tangled so closely to me that we were vines
or underbrush together,
or hands clenched.

3.

They are cutting babies in half on bets.
The beautiful sergeant has enough money to drink
for a week.
The beautiful lieutenant can't stop betting.
The little boy whimpers
he'll be good.
The beautiful cook is gathering up meat
for the dogs.
The beautiful dogs
love it all.
Their flanks glisten.
They curl up in their warm kennels
and breathe.
They breathe.

4.

Little Sister,
you are a clot
in the snow,
blackened,
a chunk of phlegm
or puke
and there are men with faces
leaning over you with watercans

watering you!
in the snow, as though flowers would sprout
from your armpits
and genitals.

Little Sister,
I am afraid of the flowers sprouting from you

I am afraid of the silver petals
that crackle
of the stems darting
in the wind
of the roots

5.

The twilight rots.
Over the greasy bridges and factories,
it dissolves
and the clouds swamp in its rose
to nothing.
I think sometimes the slag heaps by the river
should be bodies

and that the pods of moral terror
men make of their flesh should split
and foam their cold, sterile seeds into the tides
like snow
or ash.

6.
Stacks of hair were there
little mountains
the gestapo children must have played in
and made love in and loved
the way children love haystacks or mountains

O God the stink
of hair oil and dandruff

their mothers must have thrown them into their tubs
like puppies and sent them to bed

coming home so filthy stinking

of jew's hair

of gold fillings, of eyelids

7.
Under me on a roof
a sparrow little by little
is being blown away.
A cage of bone is left,
part of its wings,
a stain.

8.

And in Germany the streetcar conductors go to work
in their stiff hats,
depositing workers and housewives
where they belong,
pulling the bell chains,
moving drive levers forward or back.

9.

*I am saying goodbye to you before our death. Dear Father:
I am saying goodbye to you before my death. We are so
anxious to live, but all is lost—we are not allowed! I am
so afraid of this death, because little children are thrown
into graves alive. Goodbye forever.*

I kiss you.

10.

Come with me, Anne.
Come,
it is awful not to be anywhere at all,
to have no one
like an old whore,
a general.

Come sit with me here
kiss me; my heart too is wounded
with forgiveness.

There is an end now.
Stay.
Your foot hooked through mine

your hand against my hand
your hip touching me lightly

it will end now
it will not begin again

Stay
they will pass
and not know us

the cold brute earth
is asleep

there is no danger

there is nothing

Anne

there is nothing

Being Alone

Never on one single pore Eternity
have I been touched by your snows

or felt your shy mouth tremble,
your breath break on me

like the white wave. I have not felt
your nakedness tear me

with hunger or your silver hands
betray me but today I promise

whatever flower of your house
should bloom I will stay

locked to its breast.
Like little fish who live

harmlessly under the bellies of sharks,
I will go where you go,

drift inconspicuously
in the raw dredge of your power

like a leaf, a bubble of carrion,
a man who has understood and does not.

from

I Am the Bitter Name

(1972)

Yours

I'd like every girl in the world to have a poem of her own
I've written for her I don't even want to make love to them all anymore
just write things your body makes me delirious your face enchants me
you are a wonder of soul spirit intelligence one for every one
and then the men I don't care whether I can still beat them all
them too a poem for them how many?
seeing you go through woods like part of the woods seeing you play piano
seeing you hold your child in your tender devastating hands
and of course the children too little poems they could sing or dance to
this is our jumping game this our seeing game our holding each other
even the presidents with all their death the congressmen and judges
I'd give them something
they would hold awed to their chests as their proudest life thing
somebody walking along a road where there's no city would look up
and see his poem coming down like a feather out of nowhere
or on the assembly line new instructions a voice sweet as lunch-time
or she would turn over a stone by the fire and if she couldn't read
it would sing to her in her body
listen! everyone! you have your own poem now
it's yours as much as your heart as much as your own life is
you can do things to it shine it up iron it dress it in doll clothes
o men! o people! please stop how it's happening now please
I'm working as fast as I can I can't stop to use periods
sometimes I draw straight lines on the page because the words
are too slow
I can only do one at a time don't die first please
don't give up and start crying or hating each other they're coming
I'm hurrying be patient there's still time isn't there? isn't there?

from

With Ignorance

(1977)

Bread

A whole section of the city I live in has been urban renewed, some of it
    torn down,

some restored to what it was supposed to have been a few hundred years
    ago.

Once you could've walked blocks without hearing English, now the
    ghettos have been cleared,

there are parks and walkways and the houses are all owned by people
    who've moved back from the suburbs.

When I lived there, at the very edge of it where the expressway is going
    in now

and the buildings are still boarded with plywood or flattened altogether,

the old market was already shuttered, the shipping depots had been
    relocated upriver

and the only person I ever saw was a grocer who lived across from me over
    his empty store.

I couldn't understand what he was doing there—it must have been years

since a customer had come in past the dead register and the icebox
    propped open with a carton,

but it was comforting to have him: he'd make his bed, sweep, cook for
    himself like a little wife

and when the constables came every week or so to tell us we were
    condemned,

he never paid attention so I didn't either. I didn't want to leave. I'd been
    in love,

I thought I was healing, for all I know I might have stayed forever in the
    grim room I was camped in

but one day some boys who must have climbed up through one of the
    abandoned tenements

suddenly appeared skidding and wrestling over the steep pitch of the old
    man's roof

and when I shouted at them to get the hell off, he must have thought I'd
    meant him:

he lurched in his bed and stopped rubbing himself with the white cream
    he used to use on his breasts.

He looked up, our eyes met, and I think for the first time he really
    believed I was there.

I don't know how long we stared at each other—I could hear the kids
    shrieking at me

and the road-building equipment that had just started tearing the skin
    from the avenue—

then his zincy fingers slowly subsided against his heart and he smiled,

a brilliant, total, incongruous smile, and even though I had no desire to,

the way afterwards I had no desire to cry when my children were born,
    but did,

sobbed, broke down with joy or some inadmissible apprehension, I
    smiled back.

It was as though we were lovers, as though, like lovers, we'd made speech
    again

and were listening as it gutted and fixed the space between us and then
    a violent,

almost physical loathing took me, for all I'd done to have ended in this
    place,

to myself, to everyone, to the whole business we're given the name life for.

I could go on with this. I could call it a victory, an exemplary triumph,
    but I'd lie.

Sometimes the universe inside us can assume the aspect of places we've
    been

so that instead of emotions we see trees we knew or touched or a path,

and instead of the face of a thought, there'll be an unmade bed, a car
    nosing from an alley.

All I know about that time is that it stayed, that something, pain or the
    fear of it,

makes me stop the wheel and reach to the silence beyond my eyes and it's
    still there:

the empty wind, the white crosses of the renewers slashed on the
    doorposts,

the last, dim layers of paint loosening from the rotted sills, drifting down.

Spit

. . . then the son of the "superior race" began to spit into the
Rabbi's mouth so that the Rabbi could continue to spit on the
Torah . . .

—THE BLACK BOOK

After this much time, it's still impossible. The SS man with his stiff hair
    and his uniform;
the Rabbi, probably in a torn overcoat, probably with a stained beard the
    other would be clutching;
the Torah, God's word, on the altar, the letters blurring under the
    blended phlegm;
the Rabbi's parched mouth, the SS man perfectly absorbed, obsessed
    with perfect humiliation.
So many years and what is there to say still about the soldiers waiting
    impatiently in the snow,
about the one stamping his feet, thinking, Kill him! Get it over with!
while back there the lips of the Rabbi and the other would have brushed
and if time had stopped you would have thought they were lovers,
so lightly kissing, the sharp, luger hand under the dear chin,
the eyes furled slightly and then when it started again the eyelashes of
    both of them
shyly fluttering as wonderfully as the pulse of a baby.
Maybe we don't have to speak of it at all, it's still the same.
War, that happens and stops happening but is always somehow right
    there, twisting and hardening us;
then what we make of God—words, spit, degradation, murder, shame;
    every conceivable torment.
All these ways to live that have something to do with how we live
and that we're almost ashamed to use as metaphors for what goes on in us

but that we do anyway, so that love is battle and we watch ourselves in love

become maddened with pride and incompletion, and God is what it is when we're alone

wrestling with solitude and everything speaking in our souls turns against us like His fury

and just facing another person, there is so much terror and hatred that yes,

spitting in someone's mouth, trying to make him defile his own meaning,

would signify the struggle to survive each other and what we'll enact to accomplish it.

There's another legend.

It's about Moses, that when they first brought him as a child before Pharaoh,

the king tested him by putting a diamond and a live coal in front of him

and Moses picked up the red ember and popped it into his mouth

so for the rest of his life he was tongue-tied and Aaron had to speak for him.

What must his scarred tongue have felt like in his mouth?

It must have been like always carrying something there that weighed too much,

something leathery and dead whose greatest gravity was to loll out like an ox's,

and when it moved, it must have been like a thick embryo slowly coming alive,

butting itself against the inner sides of his teeth and cheeks.

And when God burned in the bush, how could he not cleave to him?

How could he not know that all of us were on fire and that every word we said would burn forever,

in pain, unquenchably, and that God knew it, too, and would say nothing Himself ever again beyond this,

ever, but would only live in the flesh that we use like firewood,
in all the caves of the body, the gut cave, the speech cave:
He would slobber and howl like something just barely a man that beats
    itself again and again onto the dark,
moist walls away from the light, away from whatever would be light for
    this last eternity.
"Now therefore go," He said, "and I will be with thy mouth."

The Shade

A summer cold. No rash. No fever. Nothing. But a dozen times during
   the night I wake
to listen to my son whimpering in his sleep, trying to snort the sticky
   phlegm out of his nostrils.
The passage clears, silence, nothing. I cross the room, groping for the
   warm,
elusive creature of his breath and my heart lunges, stutters, tries to race
   away;
I don't know from what, from my imagination, from life itself, maybe
   from understanding too well
and being unable to do anything about how much of my anxiety is always
   for myself.
Whatever it was, I left it when the dawn came. There's a park near here
   where everyone who's out of work in our neighborhood comes to line
   up in the morning.
The converted school buses shuttling hands to the cannery fields in Jersey
   were just rattling away when I got there
and the small-time contractors, hiring out cheap walls, cheap ditches,
   cheap everything,
were loading laborers onto the sacks of plaster and concrete in the backs
   of their pickups.
A few housewives drove by looking for someone to babysit or clean cellars
   for them,
then the gates of the local bar unlaced and whoever was left drifted in out
   of the wall of heat
already rolling in with the first fists of smoke from the city incinerators.

It's so quiet now, I can hear the sparrows foraging scraps of garbage on
   the paths.

The stove husk chained as a sign to the store across the street creaks in
the last breeze of darkness.

By noon, you'd have to be out of your mind to want to be here: the park
will reek of urine,

bodies will be sprawled on the benches, men will wrestle through the surf
of broken bottles,

but even now, watching the leaves of the elms softly lifting toward the
day, softly falling back,

all I see is fear forgiving fear on every page I turn; all I know is every time
I try to change it,

I say it again: my wife, my child . . . my home, my work, my sorrow.

If this were the last morning of the world, if time had finally moved inside
us and erupted

and we were Agamemnon again, Helen again, back on that faint,
beginning planet

where even the daily survivals were giants, filled with light, I think I'd
still be here,

afraid or not enough afraid, silently howling the names of death over the
grass and asphalt.

The morning goes on, the sun burning, the earth burning, and between
them, part of me lifts and starts back,

past the wash of dead music from the bar, the drinker reeling on the curb,
the cars coughing alive,

and part, buried in itself, stays, forever, blinking into the glare, freezing.

With Ignorance

> With ignorance begins a knowledge the first characteristic of
> which is ignorance.
> —KIERKEGAARD

1.

Again and again. Again lips, again breast, again hand, thigh, loin and bed
    and bed
after bed, the hunger, hunger again, need again, the rising, the spasm and
    needing again.
Flesh, lie, confusion and loathing, the scabs of clear gore, the spent seed
    and the spurt
of desire that seemed to generate from itself, from its own rising and
    spasm.
Everything waste, everything would be or was, the touching, the touch
    and the touch back.
Everything rind, scar, without sap, without meaning or seed, and
    everyone, everyone else,
every slip or leap into rage, every war, flame, sob, it was there, too, the
    stifling, the hushed,
malevolent frenzy and croak of desire, again and again, the same hunger,
    same need.
Touch me, hold me, sorrow and sorrow, the emptied, emptied again,
    touched again.
The hunger, the rising, again and again until again itself seemed to be
    need and hunger
and so much terror could rise out of that, the hunger repeating itself out
    of the fear now,
that how could you know if you lived within it at all, if there wasn't
    another,

a malediction or old prayer, a dream or a city of dream or a single, fleshless, dreamless error,

whose tongue you were, who spoke with you, butted or rasped with you, but still, tongue or another,

word or not word, what could it promise that wouldn't drive us back to the same hunger and sorrow?

What could it say that wouldn't spasm us back to ourselves to be bait or a dead prayer?

Or was that it? Only that? The prayer hunting its prey, hunting the bait of itself?

Was the hunger the faith in itself, the belief in itself, even the prayer?

Was it the dead prayer?

2.

The faces waver; each gathers the others within it, the others shuddering through it

as though there were tides or depths, as though the depths, the tides of the eyes themselves

could throw out refractions, waves, shifts and wavers and each faceless refraction

could rise to waver beneath me, to shift, to be faceless again, beneath or within me,

the lying, confusion, recurrence, reluctance, the surge through into again.

Each room, each breast finding its ripeness of shadow, each lip and its shadow,

the dimming, flowing, the waver through time, through loss, gone, irredeemable,

all of it, each face into regret, each room into forgetting and absence.

But still, if there were a moment, still, one moment, to begin in or go back to,

to return to move through, waver through, only a single moment carved back from the lie

the way the breast is carved from its shadow, sealed from the dross of
   darkness
until it takes the darkness itself and fills with it, taking the breath;
if, in the return, I could be taken the way I could have been taken, with
   voice or breast,
emptied against the space of the breast as though breast was breath and
   my breath,
taken, would have been emptied into the moment, it could rise here, now,
   in that moment, the same moment.
But it won't, doesn't. The moments lift and fall, break, and it shifts, wavers,
subsides into the need again, the faceless again, the faceless and the lie.

3.

Remorse? Blame? There is a pit-creature. The father follows it down with
   the ax.
Exile and sorrow. Once there were things we lived in, don't you remember?
We scraped, starved, then we came up, abashed, to the sun, and what was
   the first word?
Blame, blame and remorse, then sorrow, then the blame was the father
   then was ourselves.
Such a trite story, do we have to retell it? The mother took back the sun
   and we . . .
Remorse, self-regard, call it shame or being abashed or trying again, for
   the last time, to return.
Remorse, then power, the power and the blame and what did we ever
   suffer but power?
The head lifting itself, then the wars, remorse and revenge, the wars of
   humility,
the blades and the still valley, the double intention, the simple tree in the
   blood.
Then exile again, even the sword, even the spear, the formula scratched
   on the sand,

even the christening, the christened, blame again, power again, but even then,

taken out of the fire at the core and never returned, what could we not sanction?

One leg after the other, the look back, the power, the fire again and the sword again.

Blame and remorse. That gives in to desire again, in to hunger again. That gives in to . . . this . . .

4.

Someone . . . Your arm touches hers or hers finds yours, unmoving, unasking.

A silence, as though for the first time, and as though for the first time, you can listen,

as though there were chords: your life, then the other's, someone else, as though for the first time.

The life of the leaves over the streetlamp and the glow, swelling, chording, under the shadows,

and the quaver of things built, one quavering cell at a time, and the song of the cell gently bedding itself in its mortar, in this silence, this first attempting.

Even the shush of cars, the complex stress of a step, the word called into the darkness,

and, wait, the things even beyond, beyond membrane or awareness, mode, sense, dream,

don't they sing, too? Chord, too? Isn't the song and the silence there, too?

I heard it once. It changed nothing, but once, before I went on, I did hear:

the equation of star and plant, the wheel, the ecstasy and division, the equation again.

The absolute walking its planks, its long wall, its long chord of laughter or grief.

I heard silence, then the children, the spawn, how we have to teach every cell how to speak,

and from that, after that, the kiss back from the speech, the touch back from the song.

And then more, I heard how it alters, how we, the speakers, the can't-live, the refuse-to,

how we, only in darkness, groaning and thrashing into the undergrowth of our eternal,

would speak then, would howl, howl again, and at last, at the end, we'd hear it:

the prayer and the flesh crying, *Why aren't you here?* And the cry back in it, *I am! I am!*

5.

Imagine dread. Imagine, without symbol, without figure, history or histories; a place, not a place.

Imagine it must be risen through, beginning with the silent moment, the secrets quieted,

one hour, one age at a time, sadness, nostalgia, the absurd pain of betrayal.

Through genuine grief, then, through the genuine suffering for the boundaries of self

and the touch on the edge, the compassion, that never, never quite, breaks through.

Imagine the touch again and beyond it, beyond either end, joy or terror, either ending,

the context that gives way, not to death, but past, past anything still with a name,

even death, because even death is a promise offering comfort, solace, that any direction we turn,

there'll still be the word, the name, and this the promise now, even with terror,

the promise again that the wordlessness and the self won't be for one
  instant the same enacting,
and we stay within it, a refusal now, a turning away, a never giving way,
we stay until even extinction itself, the absence, death itself, even death,
  isn't longed for,
never that, but turned toward in the deepest turn of the self, the deepest
  gesture toward self.
And then back, from the dread, from locution and turn, from whatever
  history reflects us,
the self grounds itself again in itself and reflects itself, even its loss, as its
  own,
and back again, still holding itself back, the certainty and belief tearing
  again,
back from the edge of that one flood of surrender which, given space,
  would, like space itself,
rage beyond any limit, the flesh itself giving way in its terror, and back
  from that,
into love, what we have to call love, the one moment before we move
  onwards again,
towards the end, the life again of the self-willed, self-created, embodied,
  reflected again.
Imagine a space prepared for with hunger, with dread, with power and
  the power
over dread which is dread, and the love, with no space for itself, no power
  for itself,
a moment, a silence, a rising, the terror for that, the space for that.
  Imagine love.

6.

Morning. The first morning of now. You, your touch, your song and
  morning, but still,
something, a last fear or last lie or last clench of confusion clings,

holds back, refuses, resists, the way fear itself clings in its web of need or
dread.

What would release be? Being forgiven? No, never forgiven, never only
forgiven.

To be touched, somehow, with presence, so that the only sign is a step,
towards or away?

Or not even a step, because the walls, of self, of dread, can never
release,

can never forgive stepping away, out of the willed or refused, out of the
lie or the fear

of the self that still holds back and refuses, resists, and turns back again
and again into the willed.

What if it could be, though? The first, hectic rush past guilt or remorse?

What if we could find a way through the fires that aren't with us and the
terrors that are?

What would be there? Would we be thrown back into perhaps or not yet
or not needed or done?

Could we even slip back, again, past the first step into the first refusal,

the first need, first blot of desire that still somehow exists and wants to
resist, wants to give back the hard,

immaculate shell of the terror it still keeps against respite and unclench-
ing?

Or perhaps no release, no step or sign, perhaps only to wait and accept.

Perhaps only to bless. To bless and to bless and to bless and to bless.

Willed or unwilled, word or sign, the word suddenly filled with its own
breath.

Self and other the self within other and the self still moved through its
word,

consuming itself, still, and consuming, still being rage, war, the fear, the
aghast,

but bless, bless still, even the fear, the loss, the gutting of word, the
gutting even of hunger,

but still to bless and bless, even the turn back, the refusal, to bless and to bless and to bless.

7.

The first language was loss, the second sorrow, this is the last, then: yours . . .

An island, summer, late dusk; hills, laurel and thorn. I walked from the harbor, over the cliff road,

down the long trail through the rocks. When I came to our house the ship's wake was just edging onto the shore

and on the stone beach, under the cypress, the low waves reassuming themselves in the darkness, I waited.

There was a light in a room. You came to it, leaned to it, reaching, touching,

and watching you, I saw you give back to the light a light more than light

and to the silence you gave more than silence, and, in the silence, I heard it.

You, your self, your life, your beginning, pleasure, song clear as the light that touched you.

Your will, your given and taken; grief, recklessness, need or desire.

Your passion or tear, step forward or step back into the inevitable veil.

Yours and yours and yours, the dream, the wall of the self that won't be or needn't be breached,

and the breach, the touch, yours and the otherness, yours, the separateness,

never giving way, never breached really, but as simple, always, as light, as silence.

This is the language of that, that light and that silence, the silence rising through or from you.

Nothing to bless or not bless now, nothing to thank or forgive, not to triumph, surrender, mean, reveal, assume or exhaust. Our faces bent to the light, and still,

there is terror, still history, power, grief and remorse, always, always the self and the other

and the endless tide, the waver, the terror again, between and beneath, but you, now,

your touch, your light, the otherness yours, the reach, the wheel, the waves touching.

And to, not wait, not overcome, not even forget or forgive the dream of the moment, the unattainable moment again.

Your light . . . Your silence . . .

In the silence, without listening, I heard it, and without words, without language or breath, I answered.

Near the Haunted Castle

Teen Gangs Fight: Girl Paralyzed By Police Bullet
—HEADLINE

This is a story. You don't have to think about it, it's make-believe.
It's like a lie, maybe not quite a lie but I don't want you to worry about it.
The reason it's got to be a lie is because you already know the truth and
    I already know it
and what difference does it make? We still can't do anything: why kill
    yourself?
So here's the story. It's like the princess and the pea, remember?
Where they test her with mattresses and a pea and she's supposed not
    to sleep
and get upset and then they'll know she's the princess and marry her?
Except in this version, she comes in and nobody believes it's her and they
    lay her down
but instead of forty mattresses do you know what they lay her on? Money!
Of course, money! A million dollars! It's like a hundred mattresses, it's
    so soft, a thousand!
It's how much you cut from the budget for teachers to give the policemen.
It's how much you take from relief to trade for bullets. Soft!
And instead of the pea, what? A bullet! Brilliant! A tiny bullet stuck in
    at the bottom!
So then comes the prince. My prince, my beauty. Except he has holsters.
He has leather and badges. And what he does, he starts tearing the
    mattresses out.
Out? Don't forget, it's a story. Don't forget to not worry, it's pretend.
He's tearing the mattresses out and then he's stuffing them in his mouth!
This wonderful prince-mouth, this story-mouth, it holds millions, billions,
and she's falling, slowly or no, the pea, the bullet, is rising,

surging like some ridiculous funny snout out of the dark down there.

Does it touch you? Oh, yes, but don't worry, this is just a fib, right?

It slides next to your skin and it's cold and it goes in, in! as though you
were a door,

as though you were the whole bedroom; in, through the backbone,
through the cartilage,

the cords, then it freezes. It freezes and the prince is all gone,

this is the sleeping, the wrong-sleeping, you shouldn't be sleeping,

the so-heaviness in the arms, the so-heaviness in the legs, don't sleep,
they'll leave you,

they'll throw you away . . . the dollars spinning, the prince leaving,

and you, at the bottom, on the no-turning, on the pea, like a story,

on the bullet, the single bullet that costs next to nothing, like one dollar.

People torture each other so they'll tell the whole truth, right?

And study the nervous systems of the lower orders to find the truth,
right?

And tell the most obviously absurd tales for the one grain of truth?

The mother puts down her book and falls asleep watching television.

On the television they go on talking.

The father's in bed, the little gears still rip through his muscles.

The two brothers have the same dream, like Blinken and Nod, like the
mayor and the president.

The sister . . . The sister . . . The heart furnace, the brain furnace, hot . . .
hot . . .

Let's go back to find where the truth is. Let's find the beginning.

In the beginning was love, right? No, in the beginning . . . the bullet . . .

Hog Heaven

for James Harvard

It stinks. It stinks and it stinks and it stinks and it stinks.
It stinks in the mansions and it stinks in the shacks and the carpeted
    offices,
in the beds and the classrooms and out in the fields where there's no one.
It just stinks. Sniff and feel it come up: it's like death coming up.
Take one foot, ignore it long enough, leave it on the ground long enough
because you're afraid to stop, even to love, even to be loved,
it'll stink worse than you can imagine, as though the whole air was meat
    pressing your eyelids,
as though you'd been caught, hung up from the earth
and all the stinks of the fear drain down and your toes are the valves
    dripping
the giant stinks of the pain and the death and the radiance.
Old people stink, with their teeth and their hot rooms, and the kiss,
the age-kiss, the death-kiss, it comes like a wave and you want to fall
    down and be over.
And money stinks: the little threads that go through it like veins through
    an eye,
each stinks—if you hold it onto your lip it goes bad, it stinks like a vein
    going bad.
And Christ stank: he knew how the slaves would be stacked into the
    holds and he took it—
the stink of the vomit and shit and of somebody just rolling over and
    plunging in with his miserable seed.
And the seed stinks. And the fish carrying it upstream and the bird
    eating the fish
and you the bird's egg, the dribbles of yolk, the cycle: the whole thing stinks.

The intellect stinks and the moral faculty, like things burning, like the
    cave under justice,

and the good quiet men, like oceans of tears squeezed into one handful,
    they stink,

and the whole consciousness, like something plugged up, stinks, like
    something cut off.

Life stinks and death stinks and god and your hand touching your face

and every breath, daring to turn, daring to come back from the stop: the
    turn stinks

and the last breath, the real one, the one where everyone troops into your
    bed

and piles on—oh, that one stinks best! It stays on your mouth

and who you kiss now knows life and knows death, knows how it would
    be to fume in a nostril

and the thousand desires that stink like the stars and the voice heard
    through the stars

and each time—milk sour, egg sour, sperm sour—each time—dirt,
    friend, father—

each time—mother, tree, breath—each time—breath and breath and
    breath—

each time the same stink, the amazement, the wonder to do this and it
    flares,

this, and it stinks, this: it stinks and it stinks and it stinks and it stinks.

from

Tar

(1983)

Combat

Ich hatte einst ein schönes Vaterland . . . Es war ein Traum.
    —HEINRICH HEINE

I've been trying for hours to figure out who I was reminded of by the
    welterweight fighter
I saw on television this afternoon all but ruin his opponent with
    counterpunches and now I have it.
It was a girl I knew once, a woman: when he was being interviewed after
    the knockout, he was her exactly,
the same rigorous carriage, same facial structure—sharp cheekbones,
    very vivid eyebrows—
even the sheen of perspiration—that's how I'd remember her, of course . . .
    Moira was her name—
and the same quality in the expression of unabashed self-involvement,
    softened at once with a grave,
almost oversensitive attentiveness to saying with absolute precision what
    was to be said.
Lovely Moira! Could I ever have forgotten you? No, not forgotten, only
    not had with me for a time
that dark, slow voice, those vulnerable eyes, those ankles finely tendoned
    as a thoroughbred's.
We met I don't remember where—everything that mattered happened
    in her apartment, in the living room,
with her mother, whom she lived with, watching us, and in Moira's
    bedroom down the book-lined corridor.
The mother, I remember, was so white, not all that old but white:
    everything, hair, skin, lips, was ash,
except her feet, which Moira would often hold on her lap to massage and
    which were a deep,

frightening yellow, the skin thickened and dense, horned with calluses
and chains of coarse, dry bunions,

the nails deformed and brown, so deeply buried that they looked like
chips of tortoiseshell.

Moira would rub the poor, sad things, twisting and kneading at them
with her strong hands;

the mother's eyes would be closed, occasionally she'd mutter something
under her breath in German.

That was their language—they were, Moira said, refugees, but the word
didn't do them justice.

They were well-off, very much so, their apartment was, in fact, the most
splendid thing I'd ever seen.

There were lithographs and etchings—some Klees, I think; a Munch—a
lot of very flat oriental rugs,

voluptuous leather furniture and china so frail the molds were surely cast
from butterflies.

I never found out how they'd brought it all with them: what Moira told
me was of displaced-person camps,

a pilgrimage on foot from Prussia and the Russians, then Frankfurt,
Rotterdam, and here, "freedom."

The trip across the war was a complicated memory for her; she'd been
very young, just in school,

what was most important to her at that age was her father, who she'd
hardly known and who'd just died.

He was a general, she told me, the chief of staff or something of "the war
against the Russians."

He'd been one of the conspirators against Hitler and when the plot failed
he'd committed suicide,

all of which meant not very much to me, however good the story was (and
I heard it often),

because people then were still trying to forget the war, it had been almost
ignored, even in school,

and I had no context much beyond what my childhood comic books had
given me to hang any of it on.

Moira was fascinated by it, though, and by their journey, and whenever
she wanted to offer me something—

when I'd despair, for instance, of ever having from her what I had to
have—it would be, again, that tale.

In some ways it was, I think, her most precious possession, and every
time she'd unfold it

she'd seem to have forgotten having told me before: each time the images
would be the same—

a body by the roadside, a child's—awful—her mother'd tried to hide her
eyes but she'd jerked free;

a white ceramic cup of sweet, cold milk in the dingy railroad station of
some forgotten city,

then the boat, the water, black, the webs of rushing foam she'd made up
creatures for, who ran beneath the waves

and whose occupation was to snare the boat, to snarl it, then . . . she didn't
know what then,

and I'd be hardly listening anyway by then, one hand on a thigh, the
other stroking,

with such compassion, such generous concern, such cunning twenty-one-
year-old commiseration,

her hair, her perfect hair, then the corner of her mouth, then, so far away,
the rich rim of a breast.

We'd touch that way—petting was the word then—like lovers, with the
mother right there with us,

probably, I remember thinking, because we weren't lovers, not really, not
that way (not yet, I'd think),

but beyond that there seemed something else, some complicity between
them, some very adult undertaking

that I sensed but couldn't understand and that astonished me as did
almost everything about them.

I never really liked the mother—I was never given anything to like—but
    I was awed by her.

If I was left alone with her—Moira on the phone, say—I stuttered, or
    was stricken mute.

It felt like I was sitting there with time itself: everything seemed somehow
    finished for her,

but there seemed, still, to be such depths, or such ascensions, to her
    unblinking brooding.

She was like a footnote to a text, she seemed to know it, suffer it, and, if I
    was wildly uneasy with her,

my eyes battering shyly in their chutes, it was my own lack, my own
    unworthiness that made it so.

Moira would come back, we'd talk again, I can't imagine what about
    except, again, obsessively, the father,

his dying, his estates, the stables, servants, all they'd given up for the
    madness of that creature Hitler.

I'd listen to it all again, and drift, looking in her eyes, and pine, pondering
    her lips.

I knew that I was dying of desire—down of cheek; subtle, alien scent—
    that I'd never felt desire like this.

I was so distracted that I couldn't even get their name right: they'd kept
    the real pronunciation,

I'd try to ape what I remembered of my grandmother's Polish Yiddish
    but it still eluded me

and Moira's little joke before she'd let me take her clothes off was that
    we'd have lessons, "Von C—" "No, Von C—"

Later, when I was studying the Holocaust, I found it again, the name,
    Von C—, in Shirer's *Reich*:

it had, indeed, existed, and it had, yes, somewhere on the Eastern front,
    blown its noble head off.

I wasn't very moved. I wasn't in that city anymore, I'd ceased long before
    ever to see them,

and besides, I'd changed by then—I was more aware of history and was
   beginning to realize,
however tardily, that one's moral structures tended to be air unless you
   grounded them in real events.
Everything I did learn seemed to negate something else, everything was
   more or less up for grabs,
but the war, the Germans, all I knew about that now—no, never: what a
   complex triumph to have a nation,
all of it, beneath you, what a splendid culmination for the adolescence of
   one's ethics!
As for Moira, as for her mother, what recompense for those awful hours,
   those ecstatic unaccomplishments.
I reformulated her—them—forgave them, held them fondly, with a
   heavy lick of condescension, in my system.
But for now, there we are, Moira and I, down that hall again, in her room
   again, both with nothing on.
I can't say what she looked like. I remember that I thought her somewhat
   too robust, her chest too thick,
but I was young, and terrified, and quibbled everything: now, no doubt,
   I'd find her perfect.
In my mind now, naked, she's almost too much so, too blond, too gold,
   her pubic hair, her arm and leg fur,
all of it is brushed with light, so much glare she seems to singe the very
   tissue of remembrance,
but there are—I can see them now and didn't then—promises of dimness,
   vaults and hidden banks of coolness.
If I couldn't, though, appreciate the subtleties, it wasn't going to hold me
   back, no, it was *she* who held me back,
always, as we struggled on that narrow bed, twisted on each other,
   mauling one another like demented athletes.
So fierce it was, so strenuous, aggressive: my thigh *here*, my hand *here*,
   lips *here*, *here*,

hers *here* and *here* but never *there* or *there* . . . before it ended, she'd have even gone into the sounds of love,

groans and whispered shrieks, glottal stops, gutturals I couldn't catch or understand,

and all this while *nothing would be happening*, nothing, that is, in the way I'd mean it now.

We'd lie back (this is where I see her sweating, gleaming with it, drenched) and she'd smile.

She is satisfied somehow. This is what she wanted somehow. Only this? Yes, only this,

and we'd be back, that quickly, in my recollection anyway, with the mother in the other room,

the three of us in place, the conversation that seemed sometimes like a ritual, eternally recurring.

How long we were to wait like this was never clear to me; my desperation, though, was slow in gathering.

I must have liked the role, or the pretense of the role, of beast, primed, about to pounce,

and besides, her hesitations, her fendings-off, were so warm and so bewildering,

I was so engrossed in them, that when at last, once and for all, she let me go,

the dismissal was so adroitly managed that I never realized until perhaps right now

that what had happened wasn't my own coming to the conclusion that this wasn't worth the bother.

It's strange now, doing it again, the business of the camps and slaughters, the quick flicker of outrage

that hardly does its work anymore, all the carnage, all our own omissions interposed,

then those two, in their chambers, correct, aristocratic, even with the old one's calcifying feet

and the younger one's intensities—those eyes that pierce me still from
   that far back with jolts of longing.
I frame the image: the two women, the young man, they, poised, gracious,
   he smoldering with impatience,
and I realize I've never really asked myself what could she, or they,
   possibly have wanted of me?
What am I doing in that room, a teacup trembling on my knee, that odd,
   barbed name mangled in my mouth?
If she felt a real affinity or anything resembling it for me, it must have
   been as something quaint—
young poet, brutish, or trying to be brutish—but no, I wasn't even that, I
   was just a boy, harmless, awkward,
mildly appealing in some ways, I suppose, but certainly with not a thing
   about me one could call compelling,
not compared to what, given her beauty and her means, she could have
   had and very well may have, for all I knew.
What I come to now, running over it again, I think I want to keep as
   undramatic as I can.
These revisions of the past are probably even less trustworthy than our
   random, everyday assemblages
and have most likely even more to do with present unknowables, so I
   offer this almost in passing,
with nothing, no moral distillation, no headily pressing imperatives
   meant to be lurking beneath it.
I wonder, putting it most simply, leaving out humiliation, anything like
   that, if I might have been their Jew?
I wonder, I mean, if I might have been an implement for them, not of
   atonement—I'd have nosed that out—
but of absolution, what they'd have used to get them shed of something
   rankling—history, it would be:
they'd have wanted to be categorically and finally shriven of it, or of that
   part of it at least

which so befouled the rest, which so acutely contradicted it with glory
and debasement.

The mother, what I felt from her, that bulk of silence, that withholding
that I read as sorrow:

might it have been instead the heroic containment of a probably reflexive
loathing of me?

How much, no matter what their good intentions (of which from her I
had no evidence at all)

and even with the liberal husband (although the generals' reasons weren't
that pure and got there very late),

how much must they have inevitably absorbed, that Nazi generation,
those Aryan epochs?

And if the mother shuddered, what would Moira have gone through with
me spinning at her nipple,

her own juices and the inept emissions I'd splatter on her gluing her to
me?

The purifying Jew. It's almost funny. She was taking just enough of me to
lave her conscience,

and I, so earnest in my wants, blindly labored for her, dismantling guilt
or racial squeamishness

or whatever it was the refined tablet of her consciousness deemed it
needed to be stricken of.

All the indignities I let be perpetrated on me while I lolled in that
luxurious detention:

could I really have believed they only had to do with virtue, maidenhood,
or even with, I remember thinking—

I came this close—some intricate attempt Moira might be making to
redeem a slight on the part of the mother?

Or might inklings have arisen and might I, in my infatuation, have gone
along with them anyway?

I knew something, surely: I'd have had to. What I really knew, of course,
I'll never know again.

Beautiful memory, most precious and most treacherous sister: what temples must we build for you.

And even then, how belatedly you open to us; even then, with what exuberance you cross us.

Tar

The first morning of Three Mile Island: those first disquieting, uncertain,
    mystifying hours.
All morning a crew of workmen have been tearing the old decrepit roof
    off our building,
and all morning, trying to distract myself, I've been wandering out to
    watch them
as they hack away the leaden layers of asbestos paper and disassemble the
    disintegrating drains.
After half a night of listening to the news, wondering how to know a
    hundred miles downwind
if and when to make a run for it and where, then a coming bolt awake at
    seven
when the roofers we've been waiting for since winter sent their ladders
    shrieking up our wall,
we still know less than nothing: the utility company continues making
    little of the accident,
the slick federal spokesmen still have their evasions in some semblance
    of order.
Surely we suspect now we're being lied to, but in the meantime, there are
    the roofers,
setting winch-frames, sledging rounds of tar apart, and there I am, on the
    curb across, gawking.

I never realized what brutal work it is, how matter-of-factly and
    harrowingly dangerous.
The ladders flex and quiver, things skid from the edge, the materials are
    bulky and recalcitrant.

When the rusty, antique nails are levered out, their heads pull off; the underroofing crumbles.

Even the battered little furnace, roaring along as patient as a donkey, chokes and clogs,

a dense, malignant smoke shoots up, and someone has to fiddle with a cock, then hammer it,

before the gush and stench will deintensify, the dark, Dantean broth wearily subside.

In its crucible, the stuff looks bland, like licorice, spill it, though, on your boots or coveralls,

it sears, and everything is permeated with it, the furnace gunked with burst and half-burst bubbles,

the men themselves so completely slashed and mucked they seem almost from another realm, like trolls.

When they take their break, they leave their brooms standing at attention in the asphalt pails,

work gloves clinging like Br'er Rabbit to the bitten shafts, and they slouch along the precipitous lip,

the enormous sky behind them, the heavy noontime air alive with shimmers and mirages.

Sometime in the afternoon I had to go inside: the advent of our vigil was upon us.

However much we didn't want to, however little we would do about it, we'd understood:

we were going to perish of all this, if not now, then soon, if not soon, then someday.

Someday, some final generation, hysterically aswarm beneath an atmosphere as unrelenting as rock,

would rue us all, anathematize our earthly comforts, curse our surfeits and submissions.

I think I know, though I might rather not, why my roofers stay so clear
to me and why the rest,
the terror of that time, the reflexive disbelief and distancing, all we should
hold on to, dims so.
I remember the president in his absurd protective booties, looking
absolutely unafraid, the fool.
I remember a woman on the front page glaring across the misty
Susquehanna at those looming stacks.
But, more vividly, the men, silvered with glitter from the shingles, clinging
like starlings beneath the eaves.
Even the leftover carats of tar in the gutter, so black they seemed to suck
the light out of the air.
By nightfall kids had come across them: every sidewalk on the block was
scribbled with obscenities and hearts.

From My Window

Spring: the first morning when that one true block of sweet, laminar, complex scent arrives

from somewhere west and I keep coming to lean on the sill, glorying in the end of the wretched winter.

The scabby-barked sycamores ringing the empty lot across the way are budded—I hadn't noticed—

and the thick spikes of the unlikely urban crocuses have already broken the gritty soil.

Up the street, some surveyors with tripods are waving each other left and right the way they do.

A girl in a gym suit jogged by a while ago, some kids passed, playing hooky, I imagine,

and now the paraplegic Vietnam vet who lives in a half-converted warehouse down the block

and the friend who stays with him and seems to help him out come weaving towards me,

their battered wheelchair lurching uncertainly from one edge of the sidewalk to the other.

I know where they're going—to the "Legion": once, when I was putting something out, they stopped,

both drunk that time, too, both reeking—it wasn't ten o'clock—and we chatted for a bit.

I don't know how they stay alive—on benefits most likely. I wonder if they're lovers?

They don't look it. Right now, in fact, they look a wreck, careening haphazardly along,

contriving, as they reach beneath me, to dip a wheel from the curb so that the chair skewers, teeters, tips, and they both tumble, the one slowly, almost gracefully sliding in stages from his seat,

his expression hardly marking it, the other staggering over him, spinning heavily down,

to lie on the asphalt, his mouth working, his feet shoving weakly and fruitlessly against the curb.

In the storefront office on the corner, Reed and Son, Real Estate, have come to see the show.

Gazing through the golden letters of their name, they're not, at least, thank god, laughing.

Now the buddy, grabbing at a hydrant, gets himself erect and stands there for a moment, panting.

Now he has to lift the other, who lies utterly still, a forearm shielding his eyes from the sun.

He hauls him partly upright, then hefts him almost all the way into the chair, but a dangling foot

catches a support-plate, jerking everything around so that he has to put him down,

set the chair to rights, and hoist him again and as he does he jerks the grimy jeans right off him.

No drawers, shrunken, blotchy thighs: under the thick, white coils of belly blubber,

the poor, blunt pud, tiny, terrified, retracted, is almost invisible in the sparse genital hair,

then his friend pulls his pants up, he slumps wholly back as though he were, at last, to be let be,

and the friend leans against the cyclone fence, suddenly staring up at me as though he'd known,

all along, that I was watching and I can't help wondering if he knows that in the winter, too,

I watched, the night he went out to the lot and walked, paced rather, almost ran, for how many hours.

It was snowing, the city in that holy silence, the last we have, when the
storm takes hold,

and he was making patterns that I thought at first were circles, then
realized made a figure eight,

what must have been to him a perfect symmetry but which, from where
I was, shivered, bent,

and lay on its side: a warped, unclear infinity, slowly, as the snow came
faster, going out.

Over and over again, his head lowered to the task, he slogged the path
he'd blazed,

but the race was lost, his prints were filling faster than he made them now
and I looked away,

up across the skeletal trees to the tall center city buildings, some, though
it was midnight,

with all their offices still gleaming, their scarlet warning beacons signaling
erratically

against the thickening flakes, their smoldering auras softening portions
of the dim, milky sky.

In the morning, nothing: every trace of him effaced, all the field pure
white,

its surface glittering, the dawn, glancing from its glaze, oblique, relentless,
unadorned.

My Mother's Lips

Until I asked her to please stop doing it and was astonished to find that
   she not only could
but from the moment I asked her in fact would stop doing it, my mother,
   all through my childhood,
when I was saying something to her, something important, would move
   her lips as I was speaking
so that she seemed to be saying under her breath the very words I was
   saying as I was saying them.

Or, even more disconcertingly—wildly so now that my puberty had
   erupted—*before* I said them.
When I was smaller, I must just have assumed that she was omniscient.
   Why not?
She knew everything else—when I was tired, or lying; she'd know I was
   ill before I did.
I may even have thought—how could it not have come into my mind?—
   that she *caused* what I said.

All she was really doing of course was mouthing my words a split second
   after I said them myself,
but it wasn't until my own children were learning to talk that I really
   understood how,
and understood, too, the edge of anxiety in it, the wanting to bring you
   along out of the silence,
the compulsion to lift you again from those blank caverns of namelessness
   we encase.

That was long afterward, though: where I was now was just wanting to
   get her to stop,

and considering how I brooded and raged in those days, how quickly my
teeth went on edge,

the restraint I approached her with seems remarkable, although her so
unprotestingly,

readily taming a habit by then three children and a dozen years old was
as much so.

It's endearing to watch us again in that long-ago dusk, facing each other,
my mother and me.

I've just grown to her height, or just past it: there are our lips moving
together,

now the unison suddenly breaks, I have to go on by myself, no maestro,
no score to follow.

I wonder what finally made me take umbrage enough, or heart enough,
to confront her?

It's not important. My cocoon at that age was already unwinding: the
threads ravel and snarl.

When I find one again, it's that two o'clock in the morning, a grim hotel
on a square,

the impenetrable maze of an endless city, when, really alone for the first
time in my life,

I found myself leaning from the window, incanting in a tearing whisper
what I thought were poems.

I'd love to know what I raved that night to the night, what those innocent
dithyrambs were,

or to feel what so ecstatically drew me out of myself and beyond . . .
Nothing is there, though,

only the solemn piazza beneath me, the riot of dim, tiled roofs and
impassable alleys,

my desolate bed behind me, and my voice, hoarse, and the sweet, alien air
against me like a kiss.

On Learning of a Friend's Illness

for James Wright

The morning is so gray that the grass is gray and the side of the white
    horse grazing
is as gray and hard as the harsh, insistent wind gnawing the iron surface
    of the river,
while far off on the other shore, the eruptions from the city seem for once
    more docile and benign
than the cover of nearly indistinguishable clouds they unfurl to insinuate
    themselves among.

It's a long while since the issues of mortality have taken me this way.
    Shivering,
I tramp the thin, bitten track to the first rise, the first descent, and, toiling
    up again,
I startle out of their brushy hollow the whole herd of wild-eyed, shaggy,
    unkempt mares,
their necks, rumps, withers, even faces begrimed with patches of the
    gluey, alluvial mud.

All of them at once, their nostrils flared, their tails flung up over their
    backs like flags,
are suddenly in flight, plunging and shoving along the narrow furrow of
    the flood ditch,
bursting from its mouth, charging headlong towards the wires at the
    pasture's end,
banking finally like one great, graceful wing to scatter down the hillside
    out of sight.

Only the oldest of them all stays with me, and she, sway-backed, over at the knees,
blind, most likely deaf, still, when I approach her, swings her meager backside to me,
her ears flattening, the imperturbable opals of her eyes gazing resolutely over the bare,
scruffy fields, the scattered pines and stands of third-growth oak I called a forest once.

I slip up on her, hook her narrow neck, haul her to me, hold her for a moment, let her go.
I hardly can remember anymore what there ever was out here that keeps me coming back
to watch the land be amputated by freeways and developments, and the mares, in their sanctuary,
thinning out, reverting, becoming less and less approachable, more and more the symbols of themselves.

How cold it is. The hoofprints in the hardened muck are frozen lakes, their rims atilt,
their glazed opacities skewered with straw, muddled with the ancient, ubiquitous manure.
I pick a morsel of it up: scentless, harmless, cool, as desiccated as an empty hive,
it crumbles in my hand, its weightless, wingless filaments taken from me by the wind and strewn

in a long, surprising arc that wavers once then seems to burst into a rain of dust.
No comfort here, nothing to say, to try to say, nothing for anyone. I start the long trek back,

the horses nowhere to be seen, the old one plodding wearily away to join
   them,
the river, bitter to look at, and the passionless earth, and the grasses
   rushing ceaselessly in place.

Waking Jed

Deep asleep, perfect immobility, no apparent evidence of consciousness
    or of dream.

Elbow cocked, fist on pillow lightly curled to the tension of the partially
    relaxing sinew.

Head angled off, just so: the jaw's projection exaggerated slightly, almost
    to prognathous: why?

The features express nothing whatsoever and seem to call up no response
    in me.

Though I say nothing, don't move, gradually, far down within, he, or
    rather not *he* yet,

something, a presence, an element of being, becomes aware of me: there
    begins a subtle,

very gentle alteration in the structure of the face, or maybe less than that,
    more elusive,

as though the soft distortions of sleep-warmth radiating from his face
    and flesh,

those essentially unreal mirages in the air between us, were modifying,
    dissipating.

The face is now more his, Jed's—its participation in the almost Romanesque
    generality

I wouldn't a moment ago have been quite able to specify, not having its
    contrary, diminishes.

Particularly on the cheekbones and chin, the skin is thinning, growing
    denser, harder,

the molecules on the points of bone coming to attention, the eyelids finer,
    brighter, foil-like:

capillaries, veins; though nothing moves, there are goings to and fro
    behind now.

One hand opens, closes down more tightly, the arm extends suddenly
full length,
jerks once at the end, again, holds: there's a more pronounced elongation
of the skull—
the infant pudginess, whatever atavism it represented, or reversion, has
been called back.
Now I sense, although I can't say how, his awareness of me: I can feel him
begin to *think*,
I even know that he's thinking—or thinking in a dream perhaps—of me
here watching him.
Now I'm aware—again, with no notion how, nothing indicates it—that
if there was a dream,
it's gone, and, yes, his eyes abruptly open although his gaze, straight
before him,
seems not to register just yet, the mental operations still independent of
his vision.
I say his name, the way we do it, softly, calling one another from a cove
or cave,
as though something else were there with us, not to be disturbed, to be
crept along beside.
The lids come down again, he yawns, widely, very consciously manifesting
intentionality.
Great, if rudimentary, pleasure now: a sort of primitive, peculiarly
mammalian luxury—
to know, to know wonderfully that lying here, warm, protected, eyes
closed, one can,
for a moment anyway, a precious instant, put off the lower specie onsets,
duties, debts.
Sleeker, somehow, slyer, more aggressive now, he is suddenly more awake,
all awake,
already plotting, scheming, fending off: nothing said but there's mild
rebellion, conflict:

I insist, he resists, and then, with abrupt, wriggling grace, he otters down
from sight,
just his brow and crown, his shining rumpled hair, left ineptly showing
from the sheet.
Which I pull back to find him in what he must believe a parody of sleep,
himself asleep:
fetal, rigid, his arms clamped to his sides, eyes screwed shut, mouth
clenched, grinning.

The Gas Station

This is before I'd read Nietzsche. Before Kant or Kierkegaard, even
    before Whitman and Yeats.

I don't think there were three words in my head yet. I knew, perhaps, that
    I should suffer,

I can remember I almost cried for this or for that, nothing special,
    nothing to speak of.

Probably I was mad with grief for the loss of my childhood, but I wouldn't
    have known that.

It's dawn. A gas station. Route twenty-two. I remember exactly: route
    twenty-two curved,

there was a squat, striped concrete divider they'd put in after a plague of
    collisions.

The gas station? Texaco, Esso—I don't know. They were just words
    anyway then, just what their signs said.

I wouldn't have understood the first thing about monopoly or imperialist
    or oppression.

It's dawn. It's so late. Even then, when I was never tired, I'm just holding on.

Slumped on my friend's shoulder, I watch the relentless, wordless misery
    of the route twenty-two sky

that seems to be filming my face with a grainy oil I keep trying to rub off
    or in.

Why are we here? Because one of my friends, in the men's room over
    there, has blue balls.

He has to jerk off. I don't know what that means, "blue balls," or why he
    has to do that—

it must be important to have to stop here after this long night, but I don't
    ask.

I'm just trying, I think, to keep my head as empty as I can for as long as
    I can.

One of my other friends is asleep. He's so ugly, his mouth hanging, slack and wet.

Another—I'll never see this one again—stares from the window as though he were frightened.

Here's what we've done. We were in Times Square, a pimp found us, corralled us, led us somewhere,

down a dark street, another dark street, up dark stairs, dark hall, dark apartment,

where his whore, his girl or his wife or his mother for all I know, dragged herself from her sleep,

propped herself on an elbow, gazed into the dark hall, and agreed, for two dollars each, to take care of us.

Take care of us. Some of the words that come through me now seem to stay, to hook in.

My friend in the bathroom is taking so long. The filthy sky must be starting to lighten.

It took me a long time, too, with the woman, I mean. Did I mention that she, the woman, the whore or mother,

was having her time and all she would deign do was to blow us? Did I say that? Deign? Blow?

What a joy, though, the idea was in those days. Blown! What a thing to tell the next day.

She only deigned, though, no more. She was like a machine. When I lift her back to me now,

there's nothing there but that dark, curly head, working, a machine, up and down, and now,

Freud, Marx, Fathers, tell me, what am I, doing this, telling this, on her, on myself,

hammering it down, cementing it, sealing it in, but a machine, too? *Why am I doing this?*

I still haven't read Augustine. I don't understand Chomsky that well. Should I?

My friend at last comes back. Maybe the right words were there all along.
Complicity. Wonder.
How pure we were then, before Rimbaud, before Blake. *Grace. Love.*
Take care of us. Please.

from

Flesh and Blood

(1987)

Hooks

Possibly because she's already so striking—tall, well dressed, very clear,
   pure skin—

when the girl gets on the subway at Lafayette Street everyone notices her
   artificial hand

but we also manage, as we almost always do, not to be noticed noticing,
   except one sleeping woman,

who hasn't budged since Brooklyn but who lifts her head now, opens up,
   forgets herself,

and frankly stares at those intimidating twists of steel, the homely leather
   sock and laces,

so that the girl, as she comes through the door, has to do in turn now
   what is to be done,

which is to look down at it, too, a bit askance, with an air of tolerant,
   bemused annoyance,

the way someone would glance at their unruly, apparently ferocious but
   really quite friendly dog.

Peace

We fight for hours, through dinner, through the endless evening, who
  even knows now what about,
what could be so dire to have to suffer so for, stuck in one another's craws
  like fishbones,
the cadavers of our argument dissected, flayed, but we go on with it, to
  bed, and through the night,
feigning sleep, dreaming sleep, hardly sleeping, so precisely never
  touching, back to back,
the blanket bridged across us for the wintry air to tunnel down, to keep
  us lifting, turning,
through the angry dark that holds us in its cup of pain, the aching dark,
  the weary dark,
then, toward dawn, I can't help it, though justice won't I know be served,
  I pull her to me,
and with such accurate, graceful deftness she rolls to me that we arrive
  embracing our entire lengths.

The Lens

Snapshots of her grandchildren and great-grandchildren are scattered on
the old woman's lap.

How are you, Ma? her son asks, then, before she answers, to the nurse:
How's she doing?

The old woman, smiling, tilts her head back, centering her son in the
thick, unfamiliar lenses.

Her head moves left, then right, farther back now, forward, then finally
she has and holds him.

She is beaming now, an impression of almost too-rapt attentiveness,
admiration, even adoration.

Do you want to eat, Ma? the son asks; the woman starts to nod and in
doing so loses him again

and has to track him again, that same, slow, methodically circular, back-
and-forth targeting in.

You want to go downstairs for lunch? the son asks, a bit impatient: Ma,
you want to get a bite?

Dawn

The first morning of mist after days of draining, unwavering heat along
  the shore: a *breath*:
a plume of sea fog actually visible, coherent, intact, with all of the quieter
  mysteries
of the sea implicit in its inconspicuous, unremarkable gathering in the
  weary branches
of the drought-battered spruce on its lonely knoll; it thins now, sidles
  through the browning needles,
is penetrated sharply by a sparrow swaying precipitously on a drop-
  glittering twiglet,
then another bird, unseen, is there, a singer, chattering, and another, long
  purls of warble,
which also from out of sight insinuate themselves into that dim, fragile,
  miniature cloud,
already now, almost with reluctance, beginning its dissipation in the
  overpowering sunlight.

Reading: Winter

He's not sure how to get the jack on—he must have recently bought the
car, although it's an ancient,

impossibly decrepit, barely holding-together Chevy: he has to figure out
how each part works,

the base plate, the pillar, the thing that hooks to the bumper, even the
four-armed wrench,

before he can get it all together, knock the hubcap off and wrestle free the
partly rusted nuts.

This all happens on a bed of sheet ice: it's five below, the coldest January
in a century.

Cars slip and skid a yard away from him, the flimsy jack is desperately,
precariously balanced,

and meanwhile, when he goes into the trunk to get the spare, a page of
old newspaper catches his attention

and he pauses, rubbing his hands together, shoulders hunched, for a full
half minute, reading.

Reading: The Gym

The bench he's lying on isn't nearly wide enough for the hefty bulk of his
    torso and shoulders.
Shielding his eyes with his sheaf of scrawled-on yellow paper from the
    bare bulb over his head,
legs lifted in a dainty V, he looks about to tip, but catches himself with
    unconscious shrugs.
Suddenly he rises—he's still streaming from his session on the Nautilus
    and heavy bag—
goes into the shower, comes back, dries off with a gray, too-small towel
    and sits to read again,
applying as he does an oily, evil-looking lotion from a dark brown bottle
    onto his legs and belly.
Next to his open locker, a ragged equipment bag, on top a paperback: *The
    Ethical System of Hume.*
The smell of wintergreen and steam-room steam; from the swimming
    pool echoes of children screaming.

Vehicle: Forgetting

The way, playing an instrument, when you botch a passage you have to
  stop before you can go on again—
there's a chunk of time you have to wait through, an interval to let the
  false notes dissipate,
from consciousness of course, and from the muscles, but it seems also
  from the room, the actual air,
the bad try has to leak off into eternity, the volumes of being scrubbed to
  let the true resume . . .
So, having loved, and lost, lost everything, the other and the possibility
  of other and parts of self,
the heart rushes toward forgetfulness, but never gets there, continuously
  attains the opposite instead,
the senses tensed, attending, the conductors of the mind alert, waiting
  for the waiting to subside:
when will tedious normality begin again, the old calm silences recur, the
  creaking air subside?

Alzheimer's: The Wife

for Renée Mauger

She answers the bothersome telephone, takes the message, forgets the message, forgets who called.

One of their daughters, her husband guesses: the one with the dogs, the babies, the boy Jed?

Yes, perhaps, but how tell which, how tell anything when all the name tags have been lost or switched,

when all the lonely flowers of sense and memory bloom and die now in adjacent bites of time?

Sometimes her own face will suddenly appear with terrifying inappropriateness before her in a mirror.

She knows that if she's patient, its gaze will break, demurely, decorously, like a well-taught child's,

it will turn from her as though it were embarrassed by the secrets of this awful hide-and-seek.

If she forgets, though, and glances back again, it will still be in there, furtively watching, crying.

Alzheimer's: The Husband

for Jean Mauger

He'd been a clod, he knew, yes, always aiming toward his vision of the
   good life, always acting on it.
He knew he'd been unconscionably self-centered, had indulged himself
   with his undreamed-of good fortune,
but he also knew that the single-mindedness with which he'd attended to
   his passions, needs and whims,
and which must have seemed to others the grossest sort of egotism, was
   also what was really at the base
of how he'd almost offhandedly worked out the intuitions and moves
   which had brought him here,
and this wasn't all that different: to spend his long anticipated retirement
   learning to cook,
clean house, dress her, even to apply her makeup, wasn't any sort of
   secular saintliness—
that would be belittling—it was just the next necessity he saw himself as
   being called to.

Even So

Though she's seventy-four, has three children, five grown grandchildren
    (one already pregnant),
though she married and watched two men die, ran a good business—
    camping goods, tents,
not established and left to her by either of the husbands: it was her idea
    and her doing—
lived in three cities, and, since retiring, has spent a good part of the time
    traveling:
Europe, Mexico, even China, at the same time as Arthur Miller (though
    she didn't see him),
even so, when the nice young driver of their bus, starting out that day
    from Amsterdam,
asks her if she'd like to sit beside him in the jump seat where the ill tour
    guide should sit,
she's flattered and flustered and for a reason she's surprised about, feels
    herself being proud.

The Prodigy

for Elizabeth Bishop

Though no shyer than the others—while her pitch is being checked she
beams out at the audience,
one ear sticking through her fine, straight, dark hair, Nabokov would
surely say "deliciously"—
she's younger, slimmer, flatter, still almost a child: her bow looks half a
foot too big for her.
Not when she begins to play, though: when she begins to play, when she
goes swooping, leaping,
lifting from the lumbering *tutti* like a fighter plane, that bow is fire, that
bow is song,
that bow lifts all of us, father and old uncle, yawning younger brother
and bored best friend,
and brings us all to song, to more than song, to breaths breathed for us,
sharp, indrawn,
and then, as she bows it higher and higher, to old sorrows redeemed, a
sweet sensation of joy.

The City in the Hills

Late afternoon and difficult to tell if those are mountains, soft with mist,
    off across the lake,
the day's last luminosity pale over them, or if a dense, low-lying cloudbank
    is holding there,
diffusing the dusk above the cottages scattered charmingly on the just-
    discernible far shore.
A tumultuous chimney of shrilly shrieking starlings wheeling and
    turning over the wharves
abruptly unwinds a single undulating filament that shoots resolutely and
    unwaveringly across,
and now the old white steamer with its grainy voice of sentiment and
    resignation sets off, too,
to fetch the happy-ending humans implied so richly by the tiled roofs
    against the pines behind
and by the autumn air, its biting balm sensualized now by the inhalations
    of the eager evening.

Rush Hour

Someone has folded a coat under the boy's head, someone else, an Arab
  businessman in not very good French,
is explaining to the girl, who seems to have discovered, like this, in the
  crowded Métro,
her lover is epileptic, that something must be done to keep the boy from
  swallowing his tongue:
he works a billfold between the rigidly clenched teeth as the kneeling girl
  silently looks on,
her expression of just-contained terror transfiguring her, generalizing her
  almost to the mythic,
the very image of our wonder at what can befall the most ordinary
  afternoon of early love.
The spasms quiet, the boy, his left ear scarlet from rubbing the wool,
  comes to, looks up at the girl,
and she, as the rest of us begin to move away, hesitates, then lays her
  cheek lightly on his brow.

The Storm

A dense, low, irregular overcast is flowing rapidly in over the city from
    the middle South.
Above it, the sky holds blue, with scattered, intricate conglomerations of
    higher clouds
sidling in a much more even, stately procession across the dazzling,
    unsullied azure.
Now the lower level momentarily thins, fragments, and the early sun,
    still sharply angled,
breaks through into a finer veil and simmers, edges sharp, its ardent disk
    gently mottled.
Down across the roof lines, the decorative dome of Les Invalides looms,
    intruding on all this,
and suddenly a swallow banks around its gilded slopes, heading out but
    veering quickly back
as though the firmament, figured by so many volumes now, were too
    intimidating to row out in alone.

Love: Beginnings

They're at that stage where so much desire streams between them, so
  much frank need and want,
so much absorption in the other and the self and the self-admiring entity
  and unity they make—
her mouth so full, breast so lifted, head thrown back *so* far in her laughter
  at his laughter,
he so solid, planted, oaky, firm, so resonantly factual in the headiness of
  being craved so,
she almost wreathed upon him as they intertwine again, touch again,
  cheek, lip, shoulder, brow,
every glance moving toward the sexual, every glance away soaring back in
  flame into the sexual—
that just to watch them is to feel again that hitching in the groin, that
  filling of the heart,
the old, sore heart, the battered, foundered, faithful heart, snorting
  again, stamping in its stall.

from Le Petit Salvié

for Paul Zweig
1935–1984

1.

The summer has gone by both quickly and slowly. It's been a kind of eternity, each day spinning out its endlessness, and yet with every look back, less time is left . . .

So quickly, and so slowly . . . In the tiny elevator of the flat you'd borrowed
    on the Rue de Pondicherry,
you suddenly put your head against my chest, I thought to show how
    tired you were, and lost consciousness,
sagging heavily against me, forehead oiled with sweat, eyes ghastly
    agape . . . so quickly, so slowly.
Quickly the ambulance arrives, mewling at the curb, the disinterested
    orderlies strap you to their stretcher.
Slowly at the clinic, waiting for the doctors, waiting for the ineffectual
    treatments to begin.
Slowly through that night, then quickly all the next day, your last day,
    though no one yet suspects it.
Quickly those remaining hours, quickly the inconsequential tasks and
    doings of any ordinary afternoon.
Quickly, slowly, those final silences and sittings I so regret now not having
    taken all of with you.

First Desires

It was like listening to the record of a symphony before you knew any-
  thing at all about the music,
what the instruments might sound like, look like, what portion of the
  orchestra each represented:
there were only volumes and velocities, thickenings and thinnings, the
  winding cries of change
that seemed to touch within you, through your body, to be part of you
  and then apart from you.
And even when you'd learned the grainy timbre of the single violin, the
  ardent arpeggios of the horn,
when you tried again there were still uneases and confusions left, an ache,
  a sense of longing
that held you in chromatic dissonance, droning on beyond the dominant's
  resolve into the tonic,
as though there were a flaw of logic in the structure, or in (you knew it
  was more likely) you.

from

A Dream of Mind

(1992)

The Silence

He hasn't taken his eyes off you since we walked in, although you seem
not to notice particularly.

Only sometimes, when your gaze crosses his, mightn't it leave a very tiny
tuft behind?

It's my imagination surely, but mightn't you be all but imperceptibly
acknowledging his admiration?

We've all known these things; the other, whom we've never seen before,
but whose ways we recognize,

and with whom we enter into brilliant complicities; soul's receptors
tuned and armed;

the concealed messages, the plots, the tactics so elegant they might have
been rehearsed:

the way we wholly disregard each other, never, except at the most casually
random intervals,

let our scrutinies engage, but then that deep, delicious draft, that eager
passionate appreciation . . .

I tell myself that I don't care, as I might not sometimes, when no rival's
happened by,

but I do care now, I care acutely, I just wonder what the good would be if
I told you I can see

your mild glances palpably, if still so subtly, furtively, intertwining now
with his.

I'd only be insulting you, violating my supposed trust in you, belittling
both of us.

We've spent so much effort all these years learning to care for one
another's sensitivities.

In an instant that's all threatened; your affections seem as tenuous as
when we met,

and I have to ask myself, are you more valuable to me the more that you're
at risk?

Am I to you? It's degrading, thinking we're more firmly held together by
our mutual anxiety.

If my desire is susceptible to someone else's valuations of its object, then
what am I?

Can I say that my emotions are my own if in my most intimate affection
such contaminations lurk?

Still, though, what if this time I'd guessed right, and what if I should try
to tell you,

to try to laugh about it with you, to use our union, and our hard-earned
etiquettes to mock him,

this intruder—look—who with his dream of even daring to attempt you
would be ludicrous?

There would still be risks I almost can't let myself consider: that you'd be
humoring me,

that the fierce intensity of your attraction to him would already constitute
a union with him,

I'd be asking you to lie, and doing so you'd be thrown more emphatically
into his conspiracy;

your conniving with him would relegate me to the status of an obligation,
a teary inconvenience.

This is so exhausting: when will it relent? It seems never, not as long as
consciousness exists.

Therefore, as all along I knew I would, as I knew I'd have to, I keep still,
conceal my sorrow.

Therefore, when you ask, "Is something wrong?" what is there to answer
but, "Of course not, why?"

Politics

They're discussing the political situation they've been watching evolve in
a faraway country.

He's debating intensely, almost lecturing, about fanaticism and religion,
the betrayal of ideals.

He believes he's right, but even as he speaks he knows within himself that
it's all incidental;

he doesn't really care that much, he just can't help himself, what he's really
talking about

is the attraction that he feels she feels towards those dark and passionate
young men

just now glowing on the screen with all the unimpeachable righteousness
of the once-oppressed.

He says that just because they've been afflicted isn't proof against their
lying and conniving.

What he means is that they're not, because she might find them virile,
therefore virtuous.

He says that there are always forces we don't see that use these things for
evil ends.

What he means is that he's afraid that she might turn from him towards
someone suffering,

or, as possible, towards someone who'd share with similar conviction her
abhorrence of suffering.

He means he's troubled by how *sure* she is, how her compassions are so
woven into her identity.

Isn't the degree to which she's certain of her politics, hence of her rightness
in the world,

the same degree to which she'd be potentially willing to risk herself, and
him, and everything?

Also, should she wish to justify an action in her so firmly grounded
  socioethical system,
any action, concupiscence, promiscuity, orgy, wouldn't it not only let her
  but abet her?
Sometimes he feels her dialectics and her assurance are assertions of
  some ultimate availability.
Does he really want someone so self-sufficient, who knows herself so
  well, knows so much?
In some ways, he thinks—has he really come to this?—he might want
  her knowing *nothing*.
No, not nothing, just . . . a little less . . . and with less fervor, greater
  pragmatism, realism.
More and more in love with her, touched by her, he still goes on, to his
  amazement, arguing.

When

As soon as the old man knew he was actually dying, even before anyone
   else would admit it,
he wanted out of the business, out of the miserable game, and he told
   whoever would listen,
whenever they'd listen, wife, family, friends, that he'd do it himself but
   how could he,
without someone to help, unable to walk as he was, get out of bed or up
   from the toilet himself?

At first he'd almost been funny: "Somebody comes, somebody goes," he'd
   said on the birth of a niece,
and one day at lunch, "Please pass the cream cheese," then, deadpan,
   "That's all I'll miss."
But now he's obsessed: "Why won't you help me?" he says to his children,
   ten times a day,
a hundred and ten, but what if such meddling's wrong, and aren't these
   last days anyway precious?

Still, he was wearing them down: "This is no fun," he said to a son helping
   him hobble downstairs,
and the son, knowing full well what he meant, dreading to hear what he
   meant, had to ask "What?"
so the old man, the biopsy incision still lumping the stubble of hair on
   the side of his skull,
could look in his eyes and say, if not as an accusation then nearly, "Death,
   dying: you know."

By then they knew, too, that sooner or later they'd have to give in, then
   sooner was over,

only later was looming, aphasiac, raving too late, so they held council and
    argued it out,

and though his daughter, holding on to lost hopes, was afraid, they
    decided to help him,

and told the old man, who said, "Finally, at last," and then to his daughter,
    "Don't be afraid."

On the day it would happen, the old man would be funny again: wolfing
    down handfuls of pills,

"I know this'll upset my stomach," he'd say, but for now he only asks how
    it will happen.

"You'll just sleep," he's told, and "That's great" is his answer: "I haven't
    slept for weeks."

Then "Great" again, then, serious, dry-eyed, to his weeping family: "Just
    don't tell me when."

A Dream of Mind

for Adam Zagajewski

The Method

A dream of method first, in which mind is malleable, its products as
   revisable as sentences,
in which I'll be able to extract and then illuminate the themes of being
   as I never have.
I'm intrigued—how not be?—but I soon realize that though so much
   flexibility is tempting—
whole zones of consciousness wouldn't only be reflected or referred to,
   but embodied, as themselves,
before the sense-stuff of the world is attached to them, adulterating and
   misrepresenting them—
I have only the sketchiest notion of how to incorporate this exotic and
   complicated methodology,
and when I try, something in my character resists manipulating elements
   of mind so radically.
Imagine being offered an instrument to play that violated all your
   previous aesthetic norms,
with a fleshy, tender, sensitive component, crudely sewn or soldered to an
   innocently inorganic,
and a shape that hinted at the most contradictory techniques—brute
   force, a delicate dexterity.
You know you're supposed to draw this hybrid to your breast, to try to
   coax from it its music,
but under the tension of so many formal contradictions, what actually
   would you bring forth?
Isn't this like that? I'd be dreaming dreams of dreams, hammering out
   ideas of dreams:
wouldn't anything I'd come up with have to be a monstrous mix of
   substance and intention?

Making something out of nothing; surely more than matters of order or
   proportion are at stake.
I feel myself go cold now, taken by a clarity that makes me ask if I'm not
   already in the dream,
if I'm not merely being tempted by it, in the sense that one is tempted by
   an ill desire.
What if all this theory's the equivalent of nightmare, its menace
   masquerading as philosophy?
Can mind contort itself so recklessly and not endanger its most basic
   links to common sense?
I dream a dream of method, comprehending little of the real forces or
   necessities of dream,
and find myself entangled in the dream, entrapped, already caught in
   what the dream contrived,
in what it made, of my ambitions, or of what it itself aspired to for its
   darker dreaming.

Shadows

They drift unobtrusively into the dream, they linger, then they depart,
   but they emanate, always,
an essence of themselves, an aura, of just the frequency my mind needs to
   grasp and contain them.
Sometimes, though, the identity that I sense there, the person I feel
   intimated or implied,
is so fluid and changes so rapidly and dramatically that often I hardly
   know who I'm with.
Someone is there, then they're someone from another moment of my life,
   or even a stranger.
At first I find such a volatile mutability surprisingly less agitating than
   I'd have thought,
probably because these others brought and taken away by the dream
   manifest such careless unconcern.
Before long, though, I feel apprehensive: I find that whenever someone in
   the dream changes,
I subtly alter who I am as well, so as to stay in a proper relation with this
   new arrival
who may already be somebody else, someone for whom the self I've come
   up with is obsolete.
Suddenly I'm never quite who I should be; beset by all this tenuous
   veering and blurring,
my character has become the function of its own revisions; I'm a bystander
   in my own dream.
Even my response to such flux is growing unstable; until now I've
   considered it speculatively,
but what says I'm not going to stay in this epistemologically tremulous
   state forever?

I find I'm trying to think how to stop this, but trying to think in dream means, as always,

trying to *do*, and what do now with this presence moving towards me, wavering, shifting,

now being itself, now another, webbed now in the shadows of memory, now brilliant, burning?

Am I to try to engage it, or turn back to myself to steel myself in a more pure concentration?

Even as I watch, it transfigures again; I see it, if it is it, as through ice, or a lens.

I feel a breath touch me now, but is it this breath I feel or someone's I haven't met yet,

is it a whisper I hear or the murmur of multitudes sensing each other closer within me?

How even tell who I am now, how know if I'll ever be more than the field of these interchangings?

Vocations

Blocks of time fall upon me, adhere for a moment, then move astonish-
ingly away, fleeting, dissolving,
but still I believe that these parcels of experience have a significance
beyond their accumulation,
that though they bear no evident relation besides being occasionally
adjacent to each other,
they can be considered in a way that implies consequence, what I come to
call the dream's "meaning."
Although I can't quite specify how this ostensible meaning differs from
the sum of its states,
it holds an allure, *solutions* are implied, so I keep winding the dream's
filaments onto its core.
The problem is that trying to make the recalcitrant segments of the
dream cohere is distracting;
my mind is always half following what happens while it's half involved in
this other procedure.
Also, my ideas about meaning keep sending directives into the dream's
already crowded circuits,
and soon I'm hard put keeping the whole intractable mechanism moving
along smoothly enough
to allow me to believe that at least I'm making a not overly wasteful use
of my raw materials.
Although, doesn't the notion of "use" seem questionable, too? Use how,
and to what end?
To proliferate more complexities when I haven't come to terms with
those I've already proposed?
Mightn't all of this be only a part of the mind's longing to be other or
more than it is?

Sometimes I think I'd be better off letting the dream make its own way
without butting in so,
but no, I understand the chaos I might wreak if I left off these indispens-
able cohesions.
How depressing dream can feel now, nothing in it can move, everything
is suspended, waiting,
or, worse, not waiting, going on as it's always gone on but with such
fearful, timid resolve
that I begin to wonder if all that keeps me going is my fear of randomness,
regression, chance.
It doesn't matter anymore: whatever dream meant once, whatever it
might come to mean,
I know the only way I'll ever finish with this anguish is to understand it,
and to understand
was what the dream promised, and what, with all its blundering hopes,
it promises still.

The Solid

Although I'm apparently alone, with a pleasant but unextraordinary
  feeling of self-sufficiency,
I know I'm actually a part of a group of people who for reasons the dream
  never makes clear
are unavailable to any of my senses, though I'm always aware of the
  pressure of their presence.
No matter what else I'm doing, no matter how scant the attention I pay,
  I know they're there,
only my response to being in relation with beings I can only imagine
  alters now and again.
Usually I'm comforted: this intuition seems to impart to the dream such
  stability as it has.
Immersed with my mysterious companions in an enormous, benign,
  somehow consoling solid,
all that's required is that I not carelessly set jolts out into that sensitive
  bulk of otherness.
At other, nearly simultaneous moments, I feel signals sent, intentionally
  or not, I can't tell,
which arrive to my consciousness as an irritation, almost an abrasion of
  the material of thought.
In some far corner of dream, someone wants, needs, with such vehement,
  unreasonable fervor,
that even from here I'm afflicted with what I can only believe is an
  equivalent chagrin.
I try to think of ways to send back if not reassurance then an ack-
  nowledgment of my concern,
but I realize this would require not only energy and determination but a
  discernment, a delicacy,

the mere thought of which intimidates me, reinforcing the sense I have of my ineffectiveness.

I begin to be afraid then, the dream is deteriorating; how vulnerable I am in my very connections.

Don't my worst anxieties rise out of just such ambiguous feelings of communion and debt?

I'm suddenly swamped, overwhelmed in these tangles of unasked-for sympathies and alliances.

Always then, though, through an operation whose workings I'm never forced to explain to myself,

I'm released, the limits of my selfhood are reestablished, the nascent nightmare subsides,

and I'm able to reassume the not-incongruous sense of being alone and with so many others,

with nothing asked of me more than what any reasonable dream needs for its reasonable dreaming,

and the most minor qualms as to what I may have traded for my peace of mind, and what lost.

The Charge

An insistence in dream on a succession of seemingly urgent but possibly
   purposeless tasks
to be executed for no evident reason beyond the tautological one that
   dream says they must.
The nature of these undertakings is unclear, imprecise, they can even
   change definition,
I can never find more than the most ambiguous grounds to justify my
   obsession with them.
It seems sometimes that far away in the past of the dream a shameful
   error was committed,
and that these obligations are only my share of a more general rectifica-
   tion or atonement.
Often I can't tell if what I'm doing is by any sane measure what I'm
   supposed to be doing,
or whether all my efforts are the groundwork for yet another, still more
   illogical dream.
I'm never unaware either that I'm squandering time; this undermines my
   self-assurance still more,
so, the dream still driving me through it, me still helplessly driving myself
   through the dream,
I begin to think that persisting in this will put me into a state of such
   unmanageable consternation
that everything in me will simply go awry, leaving me tearing at myself in
   rages of frustration.
How long this has been under way, I can't tell; forever, it seems, all the
   time of the dream,
but maybe because I've looked back now, it comes to me that even should
   these needs be satisfied,

their compulsions slaked, it won't have been my doing: dream will just have been my doing: dream will just
   have pitied me,

given me surcease, not the satisfaction I'd anticipated despite all, but
   deflection and distraction.

All I'm left to hope for is that something other than nostalgia or regret
   awaits me,

that I won't end up longing for my labors, yearning for the solaces of goals
   I'd never grasped,

trying to remember when the dream of finishing what can't be finished
   ended, or if it did.

The Crime

Violence in the dream, violation of body and spirit; torment, mutilation, butchery, debasement.

At first it hardly feels real, there's something ceremonial in it, something of the dance.

The barbarisms seem formulaic, restrained, they cast a stillness about them, even a calm.

Then it comes once again, the torment, the debasement, and I have to accept that it's real.

Human beings are tearing each other to pieces, their rancor is real, and so is their pain.

Violence in the dream, but I still think—something wants me to think— there are *reasons*:

ideas are referred to, ideals, propositions of order, hierarchies, mores, structures of value.

Even in dream, though, I know it's not true, I know that if reasons there are, they're ill reasons.

Even in dream, I'm ashamed, and then, though I'm frightened, I steel myself and protest.

I protest, but the violence goes on, I cry out, but the pain, the rage, the rancor continue.

Then I suddenly realize I've said nothing at all, what I dreamed was spoken wasn't at all.

I dreamed I protested, I dreamed I cried out: I was mute, there was only an inarticulate moan.

What deceived me to think I'd objected when really I'd only cowered, embraced myself, moaned?

My incompetent courage deceived me, my too-timid hopes for the human, my qualms, my doubts.

Besides the suspicion perhaps that the dream doesn't reveal the horror
but draws it from itself,
that dream's truth is its violence, that its pity masks something I don't
want to find there.
What I hear now in the dream is the dream lamenting, its sorrow, its
fear, its cry.
Caught in the reasons of dream, I call out; caught in its sorrow, I know
who I hear cry.

Shells

Shells of fearful insensitivity that I keep having to disadhere from my
heart, how dream you?

How dream away these tireless reflexes of self-protection that almost
define heart

and these sick startles of shame at confronting again the forms of fear the
heart weaves,

the certitudes and the hatreds, the thoughtless fortifications of scarred,
fearful self?

How dream you, heart hiding, how dream the products of heart foul
with egotism and fear?

Heart's dream, the spaces holding you are so indistinct and the hurt place
you lurk so tender,

that even in dream membranes veil and distort you, only fancy and
falsehood hint where you are.

How can I dream the stripping away of the petrified membranes muffling
the tremulous heart?

I reach towards the heart and attain only heart's stores of timidity, self-
hatred, and blame;

the heart I don't dare bring to my zone of knowledge for fear it will shame
me again,

afflict me again with its pettiness, coyness, its sham zeal, false pity, and
false pride.

Dream of my heart, am I only able to dream illusions of you that touch
me with pity or pride?

How dream the heart's sorrow to redeem what it contains beyond its self-
defense and disdain?

How forgive heart when the part of me that beholds heart swells so in its
pride and contempt?

Trying to dream the dream of the heart, I hide myself from it, I veil my failures and shame.

Heart, ever unworthy of you, lost in you, will I ever truly dream you, or dream beyond you?

Room

I wanted to take up room. What a strange dream! I wanted to take up as
   much room as I could,
to swell up, enlarge, crowd into a corner all the others in the dream with
   me, but why?
Something to do with love, it felt like, but what love needs more volume
   than it has?
Lust, then: its limitlessness, the lure of its ineluctable renewal—but this
   came before lust.
Fear? Yes, the others were always more real than I was, more concrete,
   emphatic: why not fear?
Though I knew that this was my dream, they were the given and I the
   eccentric, wobbling variable.
A dubious plasma, drifting among them, self-consciously sidling, flowing,
   ebbing among them,
no wonder my atoms would boil, trying to gel, and no wonder I'd
   sometimes resent them,
brood on them, trying to understand what they were, what my connection
   to them really was.
Sometimes I'd think the point of the dream was to find what of me was
   embodied in them.
What I was with them, though, what they finally were in themselves, I
   hardly could tell.
Sometimes they seemed beasts; I could see them only as beasts, captives
   of hunger and fear.
Sometimes they were angels, nearly on fire, embracing, gleaming with
   grace, gratitude, praise.
But when their lips touched, were they kissing, or gnawing the warmth
   from a maw?

So much threatening pain to each other, so much pain accomplished: no
surprise I'd think beasts.

But still, I loved them; I wasn't just jealous of them, I loved them, was of
them, and, more,

I'd grown somehow to know in the dream that part of my love meant
accounting for them.

Account for them: how, though, why? Did they account for each other,
would they for me?

That wasn't what the dream meant to be now; I loved them, I wasn't to
ask if they loved me.

The fear, the loving and being loved, the accounting for and the wish to
had all become one.

Dream, where have you brought me? What a strange dream! Who would
have thought to be here?

Beasts, angels, taking up room, the ways of duty and love: what next,
dream, where now?

History

I have escaped in the dream; I was in danger, at peril, at immediate,
    furious, frightening risk,

but I deftly evaded the risk, eluded the danger, I conned peril to think I'd
    gone that way,

then I went this, then this way again, over the bridges of innocence, into
    the haven of sorrow.

I was so shrewd in my moment of risk, so cool: I was as guileful as though
    I were guilty,

sly, devious, cunning, though I'd done nothing in truth but be who I was
    where I was

when the dream conceived me as a threat I wasn't, possessed of a power
    I'd never had,

though I had found enough strength to flee and the guileful wherewithal
    to elude and be free.

I have escaped and survived, but as soon as I think it, it starts again, I'm
    hounded again:

no innocence now, no unlikeliest way, only this frenzied combing of the
    countries of mind

where I always believed I'd find safety and solace but where now are
    confusion and fear

and a turmoil so total that all I have known or might know drags me with
    it towards chaos.

That, in this space I inhabit, something fearsome is happening, headlong,
    with an awful momentum,

is never in doubt, but that's all I can say—no way even to be sure if I'm
    victim or oppressor;

absurd after all this not to know if I'm subject or object, scapegoat,
    perpetrator, or prey.

The dream is of beings like me, assembled, surrounded, herded like creatures, driven, undone.

And beings like me, not more like me but like me, assemble and herd them, us; undo us.

No escape now, no survival: captured, subjugated, undone, we all move through dreams of negation.

Subject, object, dream doesn't care; accumulate or subtract, self as solace, self-blame.

Thou shalt, thou shalt not; thus do I, thus I do not: dream is indifferent, bemused, abstracted.

Formulation, abstraction; assembly, removal: the dream detached; exaltation, execration, denial.

The Gap

So often and with such cruel fascination I have dreamed the implacable
   void that contains dream.

The space there, the silence, the scrawl of trajectories tracked, traced, and
   let go;

the speck of matter in non-matter; sphere, swing, the puff of agglutinate
   loose-woven tissue;

the endless pull of absence on self, the sad molecule of the self in its
   chunk of duration;

the desolate grain, flake, fragment of mind that thinks when the mind
   thinks it's thinking.

So often, too, with equal absorption, I have dreamed the end of it all:
   mind, matter, void.

I'm appalled, but I do it again, I dream it again, it comes uncalled for but
   it comes, always,

rising perhaps out of the fearful demands consciousness makes for
   linkage, coherence, congruence,

connection to something beyond, even if dread: mystery exponentially
   functioned to dread.

Again, premonitions of silence, the swoop through a gulf that might be
   inherent in mind

as though mind bore in its matter its own end and the annulment of
   everything else.

Somehow I always return in the dream from the end, from the
   meaningless, the mesh of despair,

but what if I don't once, what if the corrections fail once and I can't
   recover the thread

that leads back from that night beyond night that absorbs night as night
   absorbs innocent day?

The whole of being untempered by self, the great selves beyond self all
wholly wound out;
sense neutered, knowledge betrayed: what if this is the real end of dream,
facing the darkness
and subjecting the self yet again to imperious laws of doubt and denial
which are never repealed?
How much can I do this, how often rejuvenate and redeem with such
partial, imperfect belief?
So often, by something like faith, I'm brought back in the dream; but
this, too; so often this, too.

The Knot

Deciphering and encoding, to translate, fabricate, revise; the abstract
    star, the real star;
crossing over boundaries we'd never known were there until we found
    ourselves beyond them.
A fascination first: this was why the dream existed, so our definitions
    would be realized.
Then more than fascination as we grasped how dream could infiltrate the
    mundane with its radiance.
There'd be no mundane anymore: wholly given to the dream, our
    debilitating skepticisms overcome,
we'd act, or would be acted on—the difference, if there'd been one, would
    have been annulled—
with such purity of motive and such temperate desire that outcome
    would result from inspiration
with the same illumination that the notion of creation brings when it first
    comes upon us.
No question now of fabricating less ambiguous futures, no trying to
    recast recalcitrant beginnings.
It would be another empire of determination, in which all movement
    would be movement towards—
mergings, joinings—and in which existence would be generated from the
    qualities of our volition:
intention flowing outwards into form and back into itself in intricate
    threadings and weavings,
intuitions shaped as logically as crystal forms in rock, a linkage at the
    incandescent core,
knots of purpose we would touch into as surely as we touch the rippling
    lattice of a song.

No working out of what we used to call identity; our consummations
    would consist of acts,

of participating in a consciousness that wouldn't need, because it grew
    from such pure need,

acknowledgment or subject: we'd be held in it, always knowing there
    were truths beyond it.

Cleansed even of our appetite for bliss, we'd only want to know the
    ground of our new wonder,

and we wouldn't be surprised to find that it survived where we'd known
    it had to all along,

in all for which we'd blamed ourselves, repented and corrected, and never
    for a moment understood.

The Fear

In my dream of unspecific anxiety, nothing is what it should be, nothing
acts as it should;

everything shifts, shudders, won't hold still long enough for me to name
or constrain it.

The fear comes with no premonition, no flicker in the daily surges and
currents of dream.

Momentums, inertias, then logic distends, distorts, bends in convulsive
postures of scorn.

All I hold dear rushes away in magnetic repulsion to me, ravaged as
though by a storm,

but I know that I myself am the storm, I am the force that daunts,
threatens, rages, repels.

I am like time, I gather the things of creation and drive them out from
me towards an abyss.

All I call beauty is ravaged, transcendence hauled back in a gust to
corporeal swarm.

I never believe that the part of me which is fear can raze all the rest with
such fury,

even the flesh is depleted, forsaken; I'm no longer spirit or flesh but lost
within both,

negated, forlorn, a thing the dream can capture and propel through itself
any way it desires.

Nothing to hope for now but more concrete fears that at least might
reveal their reason.

Nothing to dream but silence and forgetting; everything failing, even the
wanting to be.

You

Such longing, such urging, such warmth towards, such force towards, so
    much ardor and desire;
to touch, touch into, hold, hold against, to feel, feel against and long
    towards again,
as though the longing, urge and warmth were ends in themselves, the
    increase of themselves,
the force towards, the ardor and desire, focused, increased, the incarna-
    tion of themselves.
All this in the body of dream, all in the substance of dream; allure,
    attraction and need,
the force so consumed and rapt in its need that dream might have evolved
    it from itself,
except the ardor urges always towards the other, towards you, and
    without you it decays,
becomes vestige, reflex, the defensive attempt to surmount instinctual
    qualms and misgivings.
No qualms now, no misgivings; no hesitancy or qualifications in longing
    towards you;
no frightened wish to evolve ideals to usurp qualm, fear or misgiving, not
    any longer.
The longing towards you sure now, ungeneralized, certain, the urge now
    towards you in yourself,
your own form of nearness, the surface of desire multiplied in the need
    that urges from you,
your longing, your urging, the force and the warmth from you, the sure
    ardor blazing in you.

from A Dream of Mind (1992)

To Listen

In the dream of death where I listen, the voices of the dream keep
diminishing, fading away.

The dead are speaking, my dead are speaking, what they say seems
urgent, to me, to themselves,

but as I try to capture more clearly what I heard just moments ago, the
voices ebb and it's lost;

what's more, my impatience to know what was said seems to drive it
further out of my ken.

In the dream of death where I listen, I keep thinking my dead have a
message for me:

maybe they'll tell me at last why they must always die in the dream, live,
die, die again.

I still can't hear what they say, though; I force my senses into the silence
but nothing is there.

Sometimes I listen so hard I think what I'm waiting to hear must already
have been spoken,

it's here, its echo surrounds me, I just have to learn to bring it more clearly
within me

and I'll know at last what I never thought I would know about death and
the dead and the speech

of affection the dead speak that stays on in the sentient space between
living and after.

For the dead speak from affection, dream says, there's kindness in the
voices of the dead.

I listen again, but I still hear only fragments of the elaborate discourse
the dead speak;

when I try to capture its gist more is effaced, there are only faded words
strewn on the page

of my soul that won't rest from its need to have what it thinks it can have
    from the dead.

Something is in me like greed now, I can't stop trying to tear the silence
    away from the voices,

I tear at the actual voices, though I know what the dead bring us is not
    to be held,

that the wanting to hold it is just what condemns dream to this pained,
    futile listening,

is what brings dream finally to its end, in silence, in want, in believing
    it's lost,

only for now, my dream thinks, at least let it be only for now, my forsaken
    dream thinks,

what the dead brought, what the dead found in their kind, blurred, weary
    voices to bring.

The Covenant

In my unlikeliest dream, my dead are with me again, companions again,
    in an ordinary way;
nothing of major moment to accomplish, no stains to cleanse, no oaths
    or debts to redeem:
my dead are serene, composed, as though they'd known all along how
    this would be.
Only I look aslant, only I brood and fret, marvel; only I have to know
    what this miracle is:
I'm awed, I want to embrace my newly found dead, to ask why they had
    to leave me so abruptly.
In truth, I think, I want pity from them, for my being bereft, for my grief
    and my pain.
But my dead will have none of my sorrow, of my asking how they came
    to be here again.
They anoint me with their mild regard and evidence only the need to
    continue, go on
in a dream that's almost like life in how only the plainest pastimes of love
    accumulate worth.
Cured of all but their presence, they seem only to want me to grasp their
    new way of being.
At first I feel nothing, then to my wonder and perhaps, too, the wonder
    of the dead,
I sense an absence in them, of will, of anything like will, as though will
    in the soul
had for the dead been all given over, transfigured, to humility, resignation,
    submission.
I know without knowing how that the dead can remember the move-
    ments of will, thought willing,

the gaze fixed at a distance that doesn't exist, the mind in its endless war
with itself—

those old cravings—but the striving to will themselves from themselves
is only a dream,

the dead know what death has brought is all they need now because all
else was already possessed,

all else was a part of the heart as it lived, in what it had seen and what it
had suffered,

in the love it had hardly remarked coming upon it, so taken it was with
its work of volition.

I can hardly believe that so little has to be lost to find such good fortune
in death,

and then, as I dream again the suspensions of will I'm still only just able
to dream,

I suddenly know I've beheld death myself, and instead of the terror, the
flexions of fear,

the repulsion, recoil, impatience to finish, be done with the waiting once
and for all,

I feel the same surge of acceptance, patience, and joy I felt in my dead
rising in me:

I know that my dead have brought what I've restlessly waited all the life
of the dream for.

I wait in joy as they give themselves to the dream once again; waiting, I'm
with them again.

Light

Always in the dream I seemed conscious of myself having the dream even
as I dreamed it.

Even now, the dream moving towards light, the field of light flowing
gently towards me,

I watch myself dreaming, I watch myself dreaming and watching, I watch
both watchers together.

It almost seems that this is what dream is about, to think what happens
as it's happening.

Still, aren't there disturbing repercussions in being in such an active
relation with dream?

What about nightmare, for instance; nightmare is always lurking there
out at the edges,

it's part of dream's definition: how be so involved in the intimate work-
ings of dream

without being an accomplice of nightmare, a portion of its cause or even
its actual cause?

Doesn't what comes to me have to be my fault, and wouldn't the alternative
be more troubling still—

that I might *not* be the one engendering this havoc, that I'm only allowed
to think so,

that the nightmare itself, hauling me through its vales of anguish, is the
operative force?

What do I mean by nightmare itself, though? Wouldn't that imply a
mind here besides mine?

But how else explain all the *care*, first to involve me, then to frighten me
out of my wits?

Mustn't something with other agendas be shaping the dream; don't all
the enticements and traps

suggest an intention more baleful than any I'd have for visiting such
mayhem on myself?

And if this isn't the case, wouldn't the alternative be as bad; that each
element of the dream

would contain its own entailment so that what came next would just do
so for no special reason?

How frivolous dream would be, then: either way, though, so much
subjugation, so little choice.

Either way, isn't the real nightmare my having so little power, *even over
my own consciousness?*

Sometimes, when I arrive in dream here, when I arrive nearly over-
whelmed with uncertainty here,

I feel a compulsion to renounce what so confounds me, to abdicate,
surrender, but to what?

I don't even know if my despair might not be another deception the
devious dream is proposing.

At last, sometimes, perhaps driven to this, perhaps falling upon it in
exhaustion or resignation,

I try to recapture how I once dreamed, innocently, with no thought of
being beside or beyond:

I imagine myself in that healing accord I still somehow believe must
precede or succeed dream.

My vigilance never flags, though; I behold the infernal beholder, I behold
the uncanny beheld,

this mind streaming through me, its turbulent stillness, its murmur,
inexorable, beguiling.

from

The Vigil

(1997)

My Fly

for Erving Goffman, 1922–1982

One of those great, garishly emerald flies that always look freshly
  generated from fresh excrement
and who maneuver through our airspace with a deft intentionality that
  makes them seem to think,
materializes just above my desk, then vanishes, his dense, abrasive buzz
  sucked in after him.

I wait, imagine him, hidden somewhere, waiting, too, then think, who
  knows why, of you—
don't laugh—that he's a messenger from you, or that you yourself (you'd
  howl at this),
ten years afterwards have let yourself be incarnated as this pestering
  anti-angel.

Now he, or you, abruptly reappears, with a weightless pounce alighting
  near my hand.
I lean down close, and though he has to sense my looming presence, he
  patiently attends,
as though my study of him had become an element of his own
  observations—maybe it is you!

Joy! To be together, even for a time! Yes, tilt your fuselage, turn it towards
  the light,
aim the thousand lenses of your eyes back up at me: how I've missed the
  layers of your attention,
how often been bereft without your gift for sniffing out pretentiousness
  and moral sham.

Why would you come back, though? Was that other radiance not
  intricate enough to parse?
Did you find yourself in some monotonous century hovering down the
  tidy queue of creatures
waiting to experience again the eternally unlikely bliss of being matter
  and extension?
You lift, you land—you're rushed, I know; the interval in all our terminals
  is much too short.
Now you hurl against the window, skid and jitter on the pane: I open it
  and step aside
and follow for one final moment of felicity your brilliant ardent atom
  swerving through.

Instinct

Although he's apparently the youngest (his little Rasta-beard is barely down and feathers),

most casually connected (he hardly glances at the girl he's with, though she might be his wife),

half-sloshed (or more than half) on picnic-whiskey teenaged father, when his little son,

two or so, tumbles from the slide, hard enough to scare himself, hard enough to make him cry,

really cry, not partly cry, not pretend the fright for what must be some scarce attention,

but really let it out, let loudly be revealed the fear of having been so close to real fear,

he, the father, knows just how quickly he should pick the child up, then how firmly hold it,

fit its head into the muscled socket of his shoulder, rub its back, croon and whisper to it,

and finally pull away a little, about a head's length, looking, still concerned, into its eyes,

then smiling, broadly, brightly, as though something had been shared, something of importance,

not dreadful, or not very, not at least now that it's past, but rather something . . . funny,

funny, yes, it was funny, wasn't it, to fall and cry like that, though one certainly can understand,

we've all had glimpses of a premonition of the anguish out there, you're better now, though,

aren't you, why don't you go back and try again, I'll watch you, maybe have another drink,

yes, my son, my love, I'll go back and be myself now: you go be the person you are, too.

Garden (Symbols)

A garden I usually never would visit; oaks, roses, the scent of roses I
    usually wouldn't remark
but do now, in a moment for no reason suddenly unlike any other,
    numinous, limpid, abundant,
whose serenity lifts and enfolds me, as a swirl of breeze lifts the leaves
    and enfolds them.

Nothing ever like this, not even love, though there's no need to measure,
    no need to compare:
for once not to be waiting, to be in the world as time moves through and
    across me,
to exult in this fragrant light given to me, in this flow of warmth given to
    me and the world.

Then, on my hand beside me on the bench, something, I thought
    somebody else's hand, alighted;
I flinched it off, and saw—sorrow!—a warbler, gray, black, yellow, in
    flight already away.
It stopped near me in a shrub, though, and waited, as though unstartled,
    as though unafraid,

as though to tell me my reflex of fear was no failure, that if I believed I
    had lost something,
I was wrong, because nothing can be lost, of the self, of a lifetime of
    bringing forth selves.
Then it was gone, its branch springing back empty: still oak, though, still
    rose, still world.

Realms

Often I have thought that after my death, not in death's void as we
usually think it,
but in some simpler after-realm of the mind, it will be given to me to
transport myself
through all space and all history, to behold whatever and converse with
whomever I wish.

Sometimes I might be an actual presence, a traveler listening at the edge
of the crowd;
at other times I'd have no physical being; I'd move unseen but seeing
through palace or slum.
Sophocles, Shakespeare, Bach! Grandfathers! Homo erectus! The
universe bursting into being!

Now, though, as I wake, caught by some imprecise longing, you in the
darkness beside me,
your warmth flowing gently against me, it comes to me that in all my
after-death doings,
I see myself as alone, always alone, and I'm suddenly stranded, forsaken,
desperate, lost.

To propel myself through those limitless reaches without you! Never! Be
with me, come!
Babylon, Egypt, Lascaux, the new seas boiling up life; Dante, Delphi,
Magyars and Mayans!
Wait, though, it must be actually you, not my imagination of you,
however real: for myself,

mind would suffice, no matter if all were one of time's terrible toys, but I
    must have you,
as you are, the unquenchable fire of your presence, otherwise death truly
    would triumph.
Quickly, never mind death, never mind mute, oblivious, onrushing time:
    wake, hold me!

The Bed

Beds squalling, squealing, muffled in hush; beds pitching, leaping, immobile as mountains;
beds wide as a prairie, strait as a gate, as narrow as the plank of a ship to be walked.

I squalled, I squealed, I swooped and pitched; I covered my eyes and fell from the plank.

Beds proud, beds preening, beds timid and tense; vanquished beds wishing only to vanquish;
neat little beds barely scented and dented, beds so disused you cranked them to start them.

I admired, sang praises, flattered, adored: I sighed and submitted, solaced, comforted, cranked.

Procrustean beds with consciences sharpened like razors slicing the darkness above you;
beds like the labors of Hercules, stables and serpents; Samson blinded, Noah in horror.

Blind with desire, I wakened in horror, in toil, in bondage, my conscience in tatters.

Beds sobbing, beds sorry, beds pleading, beds mournful with histories that amplified yours,
so you knelled through their dolorous echoes as through the depths of your own dementias.

I echoed, I knelled, I sobbed and repented, I bandaged the wrists, sighed for embryos lost.

A nation of beds, a cosmos, then, how could it still happen, the bed at the end of the world,
as welcoming as the world, ark, fortress, light and delight, the other beds all forgiven, forgiving.

A bed that sang through the darkness and woke in song as though world itself had just wakened;
two beds fitted together as one; bed of peace, patience, arrival, bed of unwaning ardor.

Grace

Almost as good as her passion, I'll think, almost as good as her presence, her physical grace,

almost as good as making love with her, I'll think in my last aching breath before last,

my glimpse before last of the light, were her good will and good wit, the steadiness of her affections.

Almost, I'll think, sliding away on my sleigh of departure, the rind of my consciousness thinning,

the fear of losing myself, of—worse—losing her, subsiding as I think, hope it must,

almost as good as her beauty, her glow, was the music of her thought, her voice and laughter.

Almost as good as kissing her, being kissed back, I hope I'll have strength still to think,

was watching her as she worked or read, was beholding her selfless sympathy for son, friend, sister,

even was feeling her anger, sometimes, rarely, lift against me, then be forgotten, put aside.

Almost, I'll think, as good as our unlikely coming together, was our constant, mostly unspoken debate

as to whether good in the world was good in itself, or (my side) only the absence of evil:

no need to say how much how we lived was shaped by her bright spirit, her humor and hope.

Almost as good as living at all—improbable gift—was watching her once cross our room,

the reflections of night rain she'd risen to close the window against flaring
across her,

doubling her light, then feeling her come back to bed, reaching to find
and embrace me,

as I'll hope she'll be there to embrace me as I sail away on that last voyage
out of myself,

that last passage out of her presence, though her presence, I'll think, will
endure,

as firmly as ever, as good even now, I'll think in that lull before last,
almost as ever.

Exterior: Day

Two actors are awkwardly muscling a coffin out of a doorway draped in
   black funeral hangings;
a third sobs, unconvincingly though: the director cries "Cut!" and they
   set up again.

Just then an old woman, blind, turns the corner; guiding herself down
   the side of the building,
she touches the velvet awning and visibly startles: has someone died and
   she not been told?

You can almost see her in her mind move through the entrance, and feel
   her way up the stairs,
knocking, trying doors—who might be missing?—but out here
   everything holds.

For a long moment no one knows what to do: the actors fidget, the
   cameraman looks away;
the woman must be aware that the street is unnaturally quiet, but she
   still doesn't move.

It begins to seem like a contest, an agon; illusion and truth: crew,
   onlookers, and woman;
her hand still raised, caught in the cloth, her vast, uninhabited gaze
   sweeping across us.

Time: 1972

As a child, in the half-dark, as you wait on the edge of her bed for her to sleep,
will lift her hand to your face and move it over your brow, cheeks, the orbits of your eyes,
as though she'd never quite seen you before, or really remarked you, or never like this,
and you're taken for a time out of your own world into hers, her world of new wonder,
and are touched by her wonder, her frank, forthright apprehending, gentle and knowing,
somehow already knowing, creating itself—you can feel it—in this outflow of bestowal,

so, sometimes, in the sometimes somber halls of memory, your life as you've known it,
in the only way you can know it, in these disparate, unpredictable upsurges of mind,
gathers itself, gathers what seem like the minds behind mind that shimmer within mind,
and turns back on itself, suspending itself, caught in the marvel of memory and time,
and, as the child's mind, so long ago now, engendered itself in attachment's touch and bestowal,
life itself now seems engendered from so much enduring attachment, so much bestowal.

Time: 1978

1.

What could be more endearing, on a long, too quiet, lonely evening in an
    unfamiliar house,

than, on the table before us, Jed's sneakers, which, finally, at eleven
    o'clock, I notice,

tipped on their sides, still tied, the soles barely scuffed since we just
    bought them today,

or rather submitted to Jed's picking them out, to his absolutely having to
    have them,

the least practical pair, but the first thing besides toys he's ever cared so
    much about,

and which, despite their impossible laces and horrible color, he
    passionately wanted, *desired*,

and coerced us into buying, by, when we made him try on the sensible
    pair we'd chosen,

limping in them, face twisted in torment: his first anguished ordeal of a
    violated aesthetic.

2.

What more endearing except Jed himself, who, now perhaps because of
    the new night noises,

wakes, and, not saying a word, pads in to sit on Catherine's lap, head on
    her breast, silent,

only his breathing, sleep-quickened, as I write this, trying to get it all in,
    hold the moments

between the sad desolation I thought if not to avert then to diminish in
    writing it down,

and this, now, my pen scratching, eyes rushing to follow the line and not
    lose Jed's gaze,

which dims with sleep now, wanders to the window—hills, brush, field
    cleft with trenches—
and begins to flutter so that I can't keep up with it: quick, quick, before
    you're asleep,
listen, how and whenever if not now, now, will I speak to you, both of
    you, of all this?

The Lover

for Michel Rétiveau

Maybe she missed the wife, or the wife's better dinner parties, but she
never forgave him,
the lover, not for having caused the husband to switch gender preference,
but for being,
she must have said, or sighed, a thousand times, so difficult to be with, so
crude, so *tiresome*.

But it was she who began to bore, the way she kept obsessively questioning
his legitimacy—
so *arch* he was, she'd say, so *bitchy*—and all after the rest of us had come
to appreciate
his mildly sardonic, often brilliant bantering, his casual erudition in so
many arcane areas.

It's true that at first he may have seemed at least a little of what she said
he was—
obstreperously, argumentatively, if wittily, abrasive—but we assigned
that to what,
considering the pack of friends' old friends with which he was faced, was
a reasonable apprehension

about being received into a society so elaborate in the intricacies of its
never articulated
but still forbiddingly solidified rituals of acceptance: he really handled it
quite graciously.
What after all did she expect of him? Shyness? Diffidence? The diffidence
of what? A bride?

from

Repair

(1999)

Ice

That astonishing thing that happens when you crack a needle-awl into a
   block of ice:
the way a perfect section through it crazes into gleaming fault-lines,
   fractures, facets;
dazzling silvery deltas that in one too-quick-to-capture instant madly
   complicate the cosmos of its innards.
Radiant now with spines and spikes, aggressive barbs of glittering light,
   a treasure hoard of light,
when you stab it again it comes apart in nearly equal segments, both faces
   grainy, gnawed at, dull.

An icehouse was a dark, low place of raw, unpainted wood,
always dank and black with melting ice.
There was sawdust and sawdust's tantalizing, half-sweet odor, which, so
   cold, seemed to pierce directly to the brain.
You'd step onto a low-roofed porch, someone would materialize,
take up great tongs and with precise, placating movements like a lion-
   tamer's slide an ice-block from its row.

Take the awl yourself now, thrust, and when the block splits do it again,
   yet again;
watch it disassemble into smaller fragments, crystal after fissured crystal.
Or if not the puncturing pick, try to make a metaphor, like Kafka's
   frozen sea within:
take into your arms the cake of actual ice, make a figure of its ponderous
   inertness,
of how its quickly wetting chill against your breast would frighten you
   and make you let it drop.

Imagine how even if it shattered and began to liquefy
the hope would still remain that if you quickly gathered up the slithery,
     perversely skittish chips,
they might be refrozen and the mass reconstituted, with precious little
     of its brilliance lost,
just this lucent shimmer on the rough, raised grain of water-rotten floor,
just this single drop, as sweet and warm as blood, evaporating on your
     tongue.

After Auschwitz

We'd wanted to make France
but by dusk we knew we wouldn't,
so in a Bavarian town
just off the autobahn,
we found a room, checked in,
and went out to look around.

The place was charming: hushed,
narrow, lamp-lit streets,
half-timbered houses,
a dark-stoned church
and medieval bridges
over a murmuring river.

I didn't sleep well, though,
and in the morning, early,
I took another stroll
and was surprised to realize
that all of it, houses,
bridges, all except

as far as I could tell
the sleeping church, were deft
replicas of what
they must have been before
the war, before the Allied
bombers flattened them.

At Auschwitz, there was nothing
I hadn't imagined beforehand.

I'd been through it in my mind
so much, so often, I felt
only unutterably weary.
All that shocked me was

to find the barracks and bleak
paths unoccupied,
and the gas and torture chambers,
and the crematoria;
so many silent spaces,
bereft, like schools in summer.

Now, in a pleasant square,
I came on a morning market;
farmers, tents and trucks,
much produce, flowers,
the people prosperous,
genial, ruddy, chatty,

and it was then there arose
before me again the barbed
wire and the bales of hair,
the laboratories and
the frozen ash. I thought
of Primo Levi, reciting

Dante to the all but dead,
then, I don't know why,
of the Jewish woman, Masha,
of whom Levi tells
how, when she'd escaped,
been informed on, caught,

and now was to be hanged
before the other prisoners,
someone called out to her,
"Masha, are you all right?"
and she'd answered, answered, answered,
"I'm always all right."

A village like a stage set,
a day's drive back
that other place which always
now everywhere on earth
will be the other place
from where one finds oneself.

Not risen from its ruins
but caught in them forever,
it demands of us how
we'll situate this so
it doesn't sunder us
between forgiveness

we have no right to grant,
and a reticence
perhaps malignant, heard
by nothing that exists,
yet which endures, a scar,
a broken cry, within.

The Dress

In those days, those days which exist for me only as the most elusive
  memory now,
when often the first sound you'd hear in the morning would be a storm
  of birdsong,
then the soft clop of the hooves of the horse hauling a milk wagon down
  your block

and the last sound at night as likely as not would be your father pulling
  up in his car,
having worked late again, always late, and going heavily down to the
  cellar, to the furnace,
to shake out the ashes and damp the draft before he came upstairs to fall
  into bed;

in those long-ago days, women, my mother, my friends' mothers, our
  neighbors,
all the women I knew, wore, often much of the day, what were called
  "housedresses,"
cheap, printed, pulpy, seemingly purposefully shapeless light cotton shifts,

that you wore over your nightgown, and, when you had to go to look for
  a child,
hang wash on the line, or run down to the grocery store on the corner,
  under a coat,
the twisted hem of the nightgown, always lank and yellowed, dangling
  beneath.

More than the curlers some of the women seemed constantly to have in
  their hair,

in preparation for some great event, a ball, one would think, that never
came to pass;
more than the way most women's faces not only were never made up
during the day,

but seemed scraped, bleached, and, with their plucked eyebrows, scarily
masklike;
more than all that it was those dresses that made women so unknowable
and forbidding,
adepts of enigmas to which men could have no access, and boys no
conception.

Only later would I see the dresses also as a proclamation: that in your
dim kitchen,
your laundry, your bleak concrete yard, what you revealed of yourself was
a fabulation;
your real sensual nature, veiled in those sexless vestments, was utterly
your dominion.

In those days, one hid much else, as well: grown men didn't embrace one
another,
unless someone had died, and not always then; you shook hands, or, at a
ball game,
thumped your friend's back and exchanged blows meant to be codes for
affection;

once out of childhood you'd never again know the shock of your father's
whiskers
on your cheek, not until mores at last had evolved, and you could hug
another man,
then hold on for a moment, then even kiss (your father's bristles white
and stiff now).

What release finally, the embrace: though we were wary—it seemed so
  audacious—
how much unspoken joy there was in that affirmation of equality and
  communion,
no matter how much misunderstanding and pain had passed between
  you by then.

We knew so little in those days, as little as now, I suppose, about healing
  those hurts:
even the women, in their best dresses, with beads and sequins sewn on
  the bodices,
even in lipstick and mascara, their hair aflow, could only stand wringing
  their hands,

begging for peace, while father and son, like thugs, like thieves, like
  Romans,
simmered and hissed and hated, inflicting sorrows that endured, the
  worst anyway,
through the kiss and embrace, bleeding from brother to brother into the
  generations.

In those days there was still countryside close to the city, farms, corn-
  fields, cows;
even not far from our building with its blurred brick and long shadowy
  hallway
you could find tracts with hills and trees you could pretend were
  mountains and forests.

Or you could go out by yourself even to a half-block-long empty lot, into
  the bushes:
like a creature of leaves you'd lurk, crouched, crawling, simplified, savage,
  alone;

already there was wanting to be simpler, wanting when they called you,
never to go back.

The Train

Stalled an hour beside a row of abandoned, graffiti-stricken factories,
the person behind me talking the whole while on his portable phone,
every word irritatingly distinct, impossible to think of anything else,
I feel trapped, look out and see a young hare moving through the sooty
    scrub;
just as I catch sight of him, he turns with a start to face us, and freezes.

Gleaming, clean, his flesh firm in his fine-grained fur, he's very endearing;
he reminds me of the smallest children on their way to school in our
    street,
their slouchy, unself-conscious grace, the urge you feel to share their
    beauty,
then my mind plays that trick of trying to go back into its wilder part,
to let the creature know my admiration, and have him acknowledge me.

All the while we're there, I long almost painfully out to him,
as though some mystery inhabited him, some semblance of the sacred,
but if he senses me he disregards me, and when we begin to move
he still waits on the black ballast gravel, ears and whiskers working,
to be sure we're good and gone before he continues his errand.

The train hurtles along, towns blur by, the voice behind me hammers on;
it's stifling here but in the fields the grasses are stiff and white with rime.
Imagine being out there alone, shivers of dread thrilling through you,
those burnished rails before you, around you a silence, immense,
    stupendous,
only now beginning to wane, in a lift of wind, the deafening creaking of
    a bough.

Depths

I'm on a parapet looking down
into a deep cleft in the earth
at minuscule people and cars
moving along its narrow bottom.
Though my father's arms are around me
I feel how far it would be to fall,
how perilous: I cringe back,
my father holds me more tightly.
Was there ever such a crevice?
No, I realized much, much later
we were on an ordinary building
looking down into a city street.

A picture book: desert sunlight,
a man and woman clad in sandals,
pastel robes, loose burnooses,
plying a material like dough,
the man kneading in a trough,
the woman throwing at a wheel.
Somehow I come to think they're angels,
in heaven, fashioning human beings.
Was there ever such a story?
No, the book, at Sunday school,
showed daily life in the Bible,
the people were just making jars.

Just jars, and yet those coils of clay,
tinted light to dark like skin,
swelled between the woman's hands

as I knew already flesh should swell,
and as I'd know it later, when,
alone with someone in the dark,
I'd close my eyes, move my hands
across her, and my mouth across her,
trying to experience an ideal,
to participate in radiances
I passionately believed existed,
and not only in imagination.

Or, with love itself, the love
that came to me so readily, so
intensely, so convincingly each time,
and each time ravaged me
when it spoiled and failed, and left
me only memories of its promise.
Could real love ever come to me?
Would I distort it if it did?
Even now I feel a frost of fear
to think I might not have found you,
my love, or not believed in you,
and still be reeling on another roof.

Tree

One vast segment of the tree, the very topmost, bows ceremoniously
 against a breath of breeze,
patient, sagacious, apparently possessing the wisdom such a union of
 space, light and matter should.

Just beneath, though grazed by the same barely perceptible zephyr, a
 knot of leaves quakes hectically,
as though trying to convince that more pacific presence above it of its
 anxieties, its dire forebodings.

Now some of the individual spreads that make up the higher, ponderous,
 stoic portion are caught, too,
by a more insistent pressure: their unity disrupted, they sway irrationally;
 do they, too, sense danger?

Harried, quaking, they seem to wonder whether some untoward response
 will be demanded of them,
whether they'll ever graze again upon the ichor with which such benign
 existences sustain themselves.

A calming now, a more solid, gel-like weight of heat in the air, in the tree
 a tense, tremulous subsiding;
the last swelling and flattening of the thousand glittering armadas of
 sunlight passing through the branches.

The tree's negative volume defines it now; the space it contains contained
 in turn by the unmoving warmth,
by duration breathlessly suspended, and, for me, by a languorous sense of
 being all at once pacified, quelled.

The Dance

A middle-aged woman, quite plain, to be polite about it, and somewhat
   stout, to be more courteous still,
but when she and the rather good-looking, much younger man she's with
   get up to dance,
her forearm descends with such delicate lightness, such restrained but
   confident ardor athwart his shoulder,
drawing him to her with such a firm, compelling warmth, and moving
   him with effortless grace
into the union she's instantly established with the not at all rhythmically
   solid music in this second-rate café,

that something in the rest of us, some doubt about ourselves, some sad
   conjecture, seems to be allayed,
nothing that we'd ever thought of as a real lack, nothing not to be ad-
   mired or be repentant for,
but something to which we've never adequately given credence,
which might have consoling implications about how we misbelieve
   ourselves, and so the world,
that world beyond us which so often disappoints, but which sometimes
   shows us, lovely, what we are.

Swifts

Why this much fascination with you, little loves, why this what feels like,
    oh, hearts,
almost too much exultation in you who set the day's end sky ashimmer
    with your veerings?
Why this feeling one might stay forever to behold you as you bank,
    swoop, swerve, soar,
make folds and pleats in evening's velvet, and pierce and stitch, dissect,
    divide,
cast up slopes which hold a beat before they fall away into the softening
    dusk?
That such fragile beings should concoct such sky-long lifting bends
    across the roofs,
as though human work counted for as little as your quickly dimming
    intersecting cries.

Tiniest dear ones, but chargers, too, gleaming, potent little coursers of
    the firmament,
smaller surely, lighter, but with that much force, that much insistence
    and enchantment;
godlings, nearly, cast upon the sky as upon a field of thought until then
    never thought,
gravity exempting from its weary weight its favorite toy, oh, you, and its
    delights, you and you,
as you hurl yourself across the tint of sinking sunlight that flows behind
    you as a wake of gold.
And the final daylight sounds you wing back to your eaves with you to
    weave into the hush,
then your after-hush which pulses in the sky of memory one last beat
    more as full dark falls.

Owen: Seven Days

for Owen Burns, born March 5, 1997

Well here I
go again into my
grandson's eyes

seven days
old and he knows
nothing logic tells me

yet when I
look into his eyes
darkish grayish blue

a whole tone
lighter
than his mother's

I feel myself almost
with a *whoosh*
dragged

into his consciousness
and processed
processed processed

his brows knit
I'm in there now
I don't know

in what form but
his gaze hasn't
faltered an instant

though still his
brows knit and
knit as though to

get just right
what I am no
what I'm thinking

as though to get
what I'm thinking
just exactly right

in perplexity perhaps
his brows knit
once again

perhaps because
of how little
inscrutability

with which the
problem of me
is presented

not "Who are you?"
but more something
like "Why?

Why are you? Out
there? Do you
know?"

then his eyelids
start to flutter
time to sleep

and once again with
something like
another *whoosh*

I'm ejected back
out into my
world

bereft? no
but for an instant
maybe just a little

lonely just a
little desolated
just for a while

utterly confounded
by the sheer
propulsive

force of
being taken
by such love

Invisible Mending

Three women old as angels,
bent as ancient apple trees,
who, in a storefront window,
with magnifying glasses,
needles fine as hair, and shining
scissors, parted woof from warp
and pruned what would in
human tissue have been sick.

Abrasions, rents and frays,
slits and chars and acid
splashes, filaments that gave
way of their own accord
from the stress of spanning
tiny, trifling gaps, but which
in a wounded psyche
make a murderous maze.

Their hands as hard as horn,
their eyes as keen as steel,
the threads they worked with
must have seemed as thick
as ropes on ships, as cables
on a crane, but still their heads
would lower, their teeth bare
to nip away the raveled ends.

Only sometimes would they
lift their eyes to yours to show

how much lovelier than these twists
of silk and serge the garments
of the mind are, yet how much
more benign their implements
than mind's procedures
of forgiveness and repair.

And in your loneliness you'd notice
how really very gently they'd take
the fabric to its last, with what
solicitude gather up worn edges
to be bound, with what severe
but kind detachment wield
their amputating shears:
forgiveness, and repair.

from

The Singing

(2003)

The Doe

Near dusk, near a path, near a brook,
we stopped, I in disquiet and dismay
for the suffering of someone I loved,
the doe in her always incipient alarm.

All that moved was her pivoting ear
the reddening sun shining through
transformed to a color I'd only seen
in a photo of a child in a womb.

Nothing else stirred, not a leaf,
not the air, but she startled and bolted
away from me into the crackling brush.

The part of my pain which sometimes
releases me from it fled with her, the rest,
in the rake of the late light, stayed.

The Singing

I was walking home down a hill near our house on a balmy afternoon
    under the blossoms
Of the pear trees that go flamboyantly mad here every spring with their
    burgeoning forth

When a young man turned in from a corner singing no it was more of a
    cadenced shouting
Most of which I couldn't catch I thought because the young man was
    black speaking black

It didn't matter I could tell he was making his song up which pleased me
    he was nice-looking
Husky dressed in some style of big pants obviously full of himself hence
    his lyrical flowing over

We went along in the same direction then he noticed me there almost
    beside him and "Big"
He shouted-sang "Big" and I thought how droll to have my height
    incorporated in his song

So I smiled but the face of the young man showed nothing he looked in
    fact pointedly away
And his song changed "I'm not a nice person" he chanted "I'm not I'm not
    a nice person"

No menace was meant I gathered no particular threat but he did want to
    be certain I knew
That if my smile implied I conceived of anything like concord between us
    I should forget it

That's all nothing else happened his song became indecipherable to me
again he arrived

Where he was going a house where a girl in braids waited for him on the
porch that was all

No one saw no one heard all the unasked and unanswered questions were
left where they were

It occurred to me to sing back "I'm not a nice person either" but I couldn't
come up with a tune

Besides I wouldn't have meant it nor he have believed it both of us knew
just where we were

In the duet we composed the equation we made the conventions to which
we were condemned

Sometimes it feels even when no one is there that someone something is
watching and listening

Someone to rectify redo remake this time again though no one saw nor
heard no one was there

Sully: Sixteen Months

One more thing to keep:
my second grandson, just
pre-speech, tripping on a toy,
skidding, bump and yowl,

and tears, real tears,
coursing down his cheeks,
until Jessie, cooing, lifts
and holds him to her,

so it's over, but as
they're leaving for home,
he and I alone a moment
in the room where he fell,

he flops down again,
to show me, look,
how it came to pass,
this terrible thing, trilling

syllables for me, no
words yet, but notes,
with hurt in them, and cries,
and that greater cry

that lurks just behind:
right here, he's saying,
on this spot precisely,
here it happened, and yes,

I answer, yes, and so
have the chance to lift him
too, to hold him, light
and lithe, against me, too.

Of Childhood the Dark

Here

Uncanny to realize one was *here*, so much
came before the awareness of being here.

Then to suspect your place here was yours only
because no one else wanted or would have it.

A site, a setting, and you the matter to fill it,
though you guessed it could never be filled.

Therefore, as much as a presence, you were a problem,
a task; insoluble, so optional, so illicit.

Then the first understanding: that you
yourself were the difficult thing to be done.

Outsets

Even then, though surely I was a "child,"
which implied sense and intent, but no power,

I wasn't what I'd learned a child should be:
I was never naïve, never without guile.

Hardly begun, I was no longer new,
already beset with quandaries and cries.

Was I a molten to harden and anneal, the core
of what I was destined to become, or was I

what I seemed, inconsequential, but free?
But if free, why quandaries, why cries?

Danger
Watch out, you might fall, as that one fell,
or fall *ill*, as he or she did, or die,

or worse, not die, be insufficient,
less than what should be your worth.

Be cautious of your body, which isn't you,
though neither are you its precise other;

you're what it feels, and the knowing
what's felt, yet no longer quite either.

Your life is first of all what may be lost,
its ultimate end to not end.

And Fear
Not lurk, not rancor, not rage, nor,
please, trapping and tearing, yet they were *there*,

from the start, impalpable but prodigious,
ever implicit. Even before anything happens,

(how know that this is what happens?)
there was the terror, the wrench and flex,

the being devoured, ingested by terror,
and the hideous inference, that from now

every absence of light would be terror,
every unheard whisper more terror.

The Lesson
One must be *right*, one's truths must
be *true*, most importantly they,

and you, must be irrefutable, otherwise
they'll lead to humiliation and sin.

Your truths will seek you, though you still
must construct and comprehend them,

then unflinchingly give yourself to them.
More than you, implying more even

than themselves, they are the single matter
for which you must be ready to lie.

The Ban
Always my awful eyes, and always
the alluring forbidden, always what I'd see

and the delirious behind or beneath; always
taboo twinned with intrigue, prohibition,

and the secret slits, which my gaze, with my assent
or without it, would slip skittering through.

Though nothing was ever as enchanting
as the anticipation of it, always my eyes

would be seeking again all they imagined,
lewd and low, might be hidden from them.

Pandora
It was clear, now that the story I'd waited
so long for had finally found me,

it was I who englobed the secrets, and the evil,
and the ruined splendor before evil,

for I guessed I'd once been in splendor.
Terrible to have coffered in myself these forebodings,

these atrocious closeds which must never
be opened, but are, ever will be.

Revealed now, though, ratified and released,
at least they were no longer just mine.

Games
The others play at violence, then so do I,
though I'd never have imagined

I'd enact this thing of attack,
of betraying, besting, rearing above,

of hand become fist, become bludgeon,
these similes of cruelty, conquest, extinction.

They, we, play at doing away with,
but also at being annulled, falling dead,

as though it were our choice, this learning
to be done away with, to fall dead.

Devout

I knew this couldn't be me, knew this holy
double of me would be taken from me,

would go out to the ravenous rocks to be dust
beneath rock, glint ashudder in dust,

but I knew I'd miss him, my swimmer in the vast;
without him was only mind-gristle and void.

Disbelief didn't drive him from me, nor the thrash
of austerities I gave him to think might be prayer.

Scorn, rather, for me, for my needing reasons to pray,
for the selves I tried to pray into being to pray.

Self-Love

No sooner had I heard of it, than I knew
I was despicably, inextricably guilty of it.

It wasn't as I'd hoped that kingdom I'd found
in myself where you whispered to yourself

and heard whispers back: that was iniquity too,
but was nothing to this; from this, I could tell,

my inept repentances would never redeem me,
so I must never trust myself again,

not the artifice I showed others, still less
that seething, sinful boil within.

First Love Lost
The gash I inflict on myself in a sludge-slow
brook in a dip in field of hornets and thorns,

I hardly remark, nor the blood spooled out behind
like a carnivore's track; it brings satisfaction,

as though I'd been tested, and prevailed. And the talon
of pain in my palm? I already know pain,

love's pain, which I know is all pain, just as I know
the river will dry, my filthy wound heal

and the wolf be driven to earth, before love,
love everlasting, will relent or release me.

Sensitive
Sensitive on a hillside, sensitive in a dusk,
summer dusk of mown clover exhaling

its opulent languor; sensitive in a gush
of ambient intimation, then inspiration, these forms

not forms bewilderingly weaving towards,
then through me, calling me forth from myself,

from the imperatives which already so drove me:
fused to sense and sensation, to a logic

other than attainment's, unknowns beckoned,
from beyond even the clover and dusk.

My Sadness
Not grounded in suffering, nor even
in death, mine or anyone else's,

it was sufficient unto itself, death and pain
were only portions of its inescapable sway.

Nor in being alone, though loneliness contained
much of the world, and infected the rest.

Sadness was the rest; engrossed in it, rapt,
I thought it must be what was called soul.

Don't souls, rapt in themselves, ravish themselves?
Wasn't I rapt? Wasn't I ravaged?

Tenses
Then seemingly all at once there was a *past*,
of which you were more than incidentally composed.

Opaque, dense, delectable as oil paint,
fauceted from a source it itself generated in you,

you were magnified by it, but it could intrude,
and weigh, like an unfathomable obligation.

Everything ending waited there, which meant
much would never be done with, even yourself,

the memory of the thought of yourself you were now,
that thought seemingly always hardly begun.

The World

Splendid that I'd revel even more in the butterflies harvesting pollen
from the lavender in my father-in-law's garden in Normandy
when I bring to mind Francis Ponge's poem where he transfigures them
to levitating matches, and the flowers they dip into to unwashed cups;
it doesn't work with lavender, but still, so lovely, matches, cups,
and lovely, too, to be here in the fragrant summer sunlight reading.

Just now an essay in *Le Monde*, on Fragonard, his oval oil sketch
of a mother opening the bodice of her rosily blushing daughter
to demonstrate to a young artist that the girl would be suitable as a "model";
the snide quotation marks insinuate she might be other than she seems,
but to me she seems entirely enchanting, even without her top
and with the painter's cane casually lifting her skirt from her ankle.

Fragonard needs so little for his plot; the girl's disarranged underslips
a few quick swirls, the mother's compliant mouth a blur, her eyes
two dots of black, yet you can see how crucial this transaction is to her,
how accommodating she'd be in working through potential complications.
In the shadows behind, a smear of fabric spills from a drawer,
a symbol surely, though when one starts thinking symbol, what isn't?

Each sprig of lavender lifting jauntily as its sated butterfly departs,
Catherine beneath the beech tree with her father and sisters, me watching,
everything and everyone might stand for something else, *be* something
    else.
Though in truth I can't imagine what; reality has put itself so solidly
    before me
there's little need for mystery . . . Except for us, for how we take the world
to us, and make it more, more than we are, more even than itself.

from

Wait

(2010)

The Gaffe

1.

If that someone who's me yet not me yet who judges me is always with
me,

as he is, shouldn't he have been there when I said so long ago that thing
I said?

If he who rakes me with such not trivial shame for minor sins now were
there then,

shouldn't he have warned me he'd even now devastate me for my
unpardonable affront?

I'm a child then, yet already I've composed this conscience-beast, who
harries me:

is there anything else I can say with certainty about who I was, except
that I, that he,

could already draw from infinitesimal transgressions complex chords of
remorse,

and orchestrate ever-undiminishing retribution from the hapless rest of
myself?

2.

The son of some friends of my parents has died, and my parents, paying
their call,

take me along, and I'm sent out with the dead boy's brother and some
others to play.

We're joking around, and words come to my mind, which to my amaze-
ment are said.

*How do you know when you can laugh when somebody dies, your brother
   dies?*

is what's said, and the others go quiet, the backyard goes quiet, everyone
   stares,
and I want to know now why that someone in me who's me yet not me
   let me say it.

Shouldn't he have told me the contrition cycle would from then be ever
   upon me,
it didn't matter that I'd really only wanted to know how grief ends, and
   when?

3.

I could hear the boy's mother sobbing inside, then stopping, sobbing then
   stopping.
Was the end of her grief already there? Had her someone in her told her
   it would end?

Was her someone in her kinder to her, not tearing at her, as mine did,
   still does, me,
for guessing grief someday ends? Is that why her sobbing stopped
   sometimes?

She didn't laugh, though, or I never heard her. *How do you know when
   you can laugh?*
Why couldn't someone have been there in me not just to accuse me, but
   to explain?

The kids were playing again, I was playing, I didn't hear anything more
   from inside.

The way now sometimes what's in me is silent, too, and sometimes, though never really, forgets.

Marina

As I'm reading Tsvetaeva's essays,
"Art in the Light of Conscience,"
stunning—"*Art, a series of answers*
to which there are no questions"—
a tiny insect I don't recognize
is making its way across my table.
It has lovely transparent wings
but for some reason they drag behind
as it treks the expanse of formica
and descends into a crack.

"*To each answer before it evaporates,*
our *question*": composed in Paris
during the difficult years of exile.
But which of her years were easy?
This at least was before the husband,
a spy, an assassin, went back,
then she, too, with her son,
to the Soviet madhouse, back . . .
"*This being outgalloped by answers,*
is inspiration . . ." Outgalloped!

Still lugging its filigreed train,
the insect emerges: fragile, distracted,
it can't even trace a straight line,
but it circumnavigates the table.
Does it know it's back where it began?
Still, it perseveres, pushing
courageously on, one inch, another . . .

"Art . . . a kind of physical world
of the spiritual . . . A spiritual world
of the physical . . . almost flesh."

One daughter, dying, at three,
of hunger, the other daughter,
that gift of a sugar-cube
in her mouth, drenched with blood . . .
"A poet is an answer . . . not to the blow,
but a quivering of the air."
The years of wandering,
the weary return, husband betrayed,
arrested, daughter in a camp . . .
"The soul is our capacity for pain."

When I breathe across it,
the bug squats, quakes, finally flies.
And couldn't she have fled again,
again have been flown? Couldn't she,
noose in her hand, have proclaimed,
"I am Tsvetaeva," and then not?
No, no time now for "then not . . ."
But *"Above poet, more than poet . . ."*
she'd already said it, already sung it:
"Air finished. Firmament now."

Cassandra, Iraq

1.

She's magnificent, as we imagine women must be
who foresee and foretell and are right and disdained.

This is the difference between us who are like her
in having been right and disdained, and us as we are.

Because we, in our foreseeings, our having been right,
are repulsive to ourselves, fat and immobile, like toads.

Not toads in the garden, who after all are what they are,
but toads in the tale of death in the desert of sludge.

2.

In this tale of lies, of treachery, of superfluous dead,
were there ever so many who were right and disdained?

With no notion what to do next? If we were true seers,
as prescient as she, as frenzied, we'd know what to do next.

We'd twitter, as she did, like birds; we'd warble, we'd trill.
But what would it be really, to *twitter*, to *warble*, to *trill*?

Is it *ee-ee-ee*, like having a child? Is it *uh-uh-uh*, like a wound?
Or is it inside, like a blow, silent to everyone but yourself?

3.

Yes, inside, I remember, *oh-oh-oh*: it's where grief
is just about to be spoken, but all at once can't be: *oh*.

When you no longer can "think" of what things like lies,
like superfluous dead, so many, might mean: *oh*.

Cassandra will be abducted at the end of her tale, and die.
Even she can't predict how. Stabbed? Shot? Blown to bits?

Her abductor dies, too, though, in a gush of gore, in a net.
That we know; she foresaw that—in a gush of gore, in a net.

Wait

Chop, hack, slash; chop, hack, slash; cleaver, boning knife, ax—
not even the clumsiest clod of a butcher could do this so crudely,
time, as do you, dismember me, render me, leave me slop in a pail,
one part of my body a hundred years old, one not even there anymore,
another still riven with idiot vigor, voracious as the youth I was
for whom everything always was going too slowly, too slowly.

It was me then who chopped, slashed, through you, across you,
relished you, gorged on you, slugged your invisible liquor down raw.
Now you're polluted; pulse, clock, calendar taint you, befoul you,
you suck at me, pull at me, barbed-wire knots of memory tear me,
my heart hangs, inert, a tag end of tissue, firing, misfiring,
trying to heave itself back to its other way with you.

But was there ever really any other way with you? When I ran
as though for my life, wasn't I fleeing from you, or for you?
Wasn't I frightened you'd fray, leave me nothing but shreds?
Aren't I still? When I snatch at one of your moments, and clutch it,
a pebble, a planet, isn't it wearing away in my hand as though I,
not you, were the ocean of acid, the corrosive in which I dissolve?

Wait, though, wait: I should tell you too how happy I am,
how I love it so much, all of it, chopping and slashing and all.
Please know I love especially you, how every morning you turn over
the languorous earth, for how would she know otherwise to do dawn,
to do dusk, when all she hears from her speech-creatures is "Wait!"?
We whose anguished wish is that our last word not be "Wait."

The Coffin Store

I was lugging my death from Kampala to Kraków.
Death, what a ridiculous load you can be,
like the world trembling on Atlas's shoulders.

In Kampala I'd wondered why the people, so poor,
didn't just kill me. *Why don't they kill me?*
In Kraków I must have fancied I'd find poets to talk to.

I still believed then I'd domesticated my death,
that he'd no longer gnaw off my fingers and ears.
We even had parties together: "Happy," said death,

and gave me my present, a coffin, my coffin,
made in Kampala, with a sliding door in its lid,
to look through, at the sky, at the birds, at Kampala.

That was his way, I soon understood, of reverting
to talon and snarl, for the door refused to come open:
no sky, no bird, no poets, no Kraków.

Catherine came to me then, came to me then,
"*Open your eyes, mon amour,*" but death
had undone me, my knuckles were raw as an ape's,

my mind slid like a sad-ankled skate, and no matter
what Catherine was saying, was sighing, was singing,
"*Mon amour, mon amour,*" the door stayed shut, oh, shut.

I heard trees being felled, skinned, smoothed,
hammered together as coffins. I heard death
snorting and stamping, impatient to be hauled off, away.

But here again was Catherine, sighing, and singing,
and the tiny carved wooden door slid ajar, just enough:
the sky, one single bird, Catherine: just enough.

Thrush

Often in our garden these summer evenings a thrush
and her two nearly grown offspring come to forage.
The chicks are fledged, the mother's teaching them
to find their own food; one learns, the other can't—
its skull is misshapen, there's no eye on one side
and the beak is malformed: whatever it finds, it drops.

It seems to regress then, crouching before the mother,
gullet agape, as though it were back in the nest:
she always finds something else for it to eat,
but her youngster's all but as large as she is,
she's feeding two of herself—she'll abandon it soon,
and migrate; the chick will doubtlessly starve.

Humans don't do that, just leave, though a young woman
I saw rushing through the train station this morning
with a Down's syndrome infant in a stroller
I thought might if she could. The child, a girl,
was giggling so hard at how splendidly fast
they were going that she'd half-fallen from her seat,

until the mother braked abruptly, hissed "Shush!"
and yanked her back into place. The baby, alarmed,
subsided but still intrepidly smiled as the mother—
she wasn't eighteen, with smudged eyeliner, scuffed shoes
and a cardboard valise—sped on, wielding carriage
and child as a battering ram through the oncoming crush.

The thrushes have been rapidly crisscrossing the lawn
in and out of the flower beds all through the long dusk,
now they leave, the rest of the birds go quiet—
I can hear someone far off calling children to bed—
and it's the turn of the bats, who materialize, vanish,
and appear again, their own after-selves, their own ghosts.

We

A basset hound with balls
so heavy they hang
a harrowing half
inch from the pavement,

ears cocked, accusingly
watches as his beautiful
mistress croons
to her silver cell phone.

She does, yes, go on,
but my, so slim-
waistedly
does she sway there,

so engrossedly does her dark
gaze drift
towards even
for a moment mine . . .

Though Mister Dog of course
sits down right
then to lick
himself, his groin of course,

till she cuts off, and he,
gathering his folds
and flab, heaves
erect to leave with her . . .

But wait, she's turning to
a great Ducati
cycle gleaming
black and chromy at the curb,

she's mounting it (that long
strong lift of flank!),
snorting it to life,
coaxing it in gear . . .

Why, she's not his at all!
No more than mine!
What was he thinking?
What was I? Like a wing,

a wave, she banks away
now, downshifts,
pops and crackles
round the curve, is gone.

How sleek she was, though,
how scrufty, how
anciently scabby
we, he and I;

how worn, how
self-devoured,
balls and all,
balls, balls and all.

All but Always

1.

If you were to possess a complicated
apparatus composed of many
intricate elements and operating
through a number of apparently unpredictable
processes, and if it were asked of you
to specify which parts of this contrivance
you had fabricated and which had come
to you already shaped and assembled,
which of its workings you'd conceived of
and set in motion yourself
and which were already under way
when it came into your possession,

2.

and if you were unable to give
an unqualified response to these questions,
but were forced to admit that you
couldn't say with certainty whether
the activities of the thing were your doing
or the result of some other agency,
or even if its real purposes
had been decided by you, or anyone,
whether there was even a reason
for its being, other than
its always having been,
as far back as you can recall,

3.

and if it came to you that this
mechanism of yours had all
but always run erratically, seemed
all but always in need of repair,
how go about repairing it
if you didn't know whether your notions
of how it worked were grounded
in more than wild surmise, if in fact
you weren't certain what to *call*
the thing—your mind, your self, your life?
What if indeed it was your mind, your self,
your life? What then? What then?

Back

First I did my thing, that's to say her thing, to her, for her,
then she did her thing, I mean my thing, to me, for me,
then we did our thing together, then again, the other way though,
then once more that way again,
then we were done, and we were at dinner,
though I desperately missed the other things now,
and said so:
"Don't you know I can't enjoy anything else now?"
and, still love-tipsy, love-stunned,
"Ever," I said: "I'll never enjoy anything else, ever again."

Except I also meant this,
I mean this being together thinking of that,
or not even her thinking—who knows what she's thinking—
I mean me thinking of that, of her, thinking and thinking,
but now that I've told her, told you, are we then,
back to, again, that?
Yes, and thank goodness I'm back there, we're back there,
I missed you out here by myself, even thinking of that,
which is why I had to do all this thinking,
to take us even in such a partial way back.

The Foundation

1.

Watch me, I'm running, watch me, I'm dancing, I'm air;
the building I used to live in has been razed and I'm skipping,
hopping, two-footedly leaping across the blocks, bricks,
slabs of concrete, plaster and other unnameable junk . . .

Or nameable, really, if you look at the wreckage closely . . .
Here, for instance, this shattered I beam is the Bible,
and this chunk of mortar? Plato, the mortar of mind,
also in pieces, in pieces in me, anyway, in my mind . . .

Aristotle and Nietzsche, Freud and Camus and Buber,
and Christ, even, that year of reading *Paradise Lost*,
when I thought, Hell, why not? but that fractured, too . . .
Kierkegaard, Hegel, and Kant, and Goffman and Marx,

all heaped in the foundation, and I've sped through so often
that now I have it by heart, can run, dance, be air,
not think of the spew of intellectual dust I scuffed up
when in my barely broken-in boots I first clumped through

the sanctums of Buddhism, Taoism, Zen and the Areopagite,
even, whose entire text I typed out—my god, why?—
I didn't care, I just kept bumping my head on the lintels,
Einstein, the Gnostics, Kabbalah, Saint This and Saint That . . .

2.

Watch me again now, because I'm not alone in my dancing,
my being air, I'm with my poets, my Rilke, my Yeats,

we're leaping together through the debris, a jumble of wrack,
but my Keats floats across it, my Herbert and Donne,

my Kinnell, my Bishop and Blake are soaring across it,
my Frost, Baudelaire, my Dickinson, Lowell and Larkin,
and my giants, my Whitman, my Shakespeare, my Dante
and Homer; they were the steel, though scouring as I was

the savants and sages half the time I hardly knew it . . .
But Vallejo was there all along, and my Sidney and Shelley,
my Coleridge and Hopkins, there all along with their music,
which is why I can whirl through the rubble of everything else,

the philosophizing and theories, the thesis and anti- and syn-,
all I believed must be what meanings were made of,
when really it was the singing, the choiring, the cadence,
the lull of the vowels, the chromatical consonant clatter . . .

Watch me again, I haven't landed, I'm hovering here
over the fragments, the remnants, the splinters and shards;
my poets are with me, my soarers, my skimmers, my skaters,
aloft on their song in the ruins, their jubilant song of the ruins.

Jew on Bridge

Raskolnikov hasn't slept. For days. In his brain, something like white.
A wave stopped in mid-leap. Thick, slow, white. Or maybe it's brain.
Brain in his brain. Old woman's brain on the filthy floor of his brain.

His destiny's closing in. He's on his way, we're given to think, though
he'll have to go first through much suffering, to punishment, then
   redemption.
Love, too. Punishment, love, redemption; it's all mixed up in his brain.

Can't I go back to my garret, to my filthy oil-cloth couch, and just sleep?
That squalid neighborhood where he lived. I was there. Whores, beggars,
derelict men with flattened noses: the police break their noses on purpose.

Poor crumpled things. He can't, though, go back to his filthy garret.
Rather this fitful perambulation. Now we come to a bridge on the Neva.
Could you see the sea from there then? I think I saw it from there.

Then, on the bridge, hanging out of the plot like an arm from a car,
no more function than that in the plot, car, window, arm, even less,
there, on the bridge, purposeless, plotless, not even a couch of his own:
   Jew.

On page something or other, chapter something, Raskolnikov sees
   JEW.
And takes a moment, a break, you might say, from his plot, from his fate,
his doom, to hate him, the Jew, loathe, despise, want him not *there*.

Jew. Not as in Chekhov's ensemble of Jews wailing for a wedding.
Not Chekhov, dear Chekhov. Dostoevsky instead, whom I esteemed

beyond almost all who ever scraped with a pen, but who won't give the Jew,

miserable Jew, the right to be short, tall, thin or fat Jew: just Jew.
Something to distract you from your shuttering tunnel of fate, your memory,
consciousness, loathing, self-loathing, knowing the slug you are.

What's the Jew doing anyway on that bridge on the beautiful Neva?
Maybe he's Paul, as in Celan. Antschel-Celan, who went over the rail of a bridge.
Oh my *Todesfugue*, Celan is thinking. The river's not the Neva, but the Seine.

It's the bridge on the Seine where Jew-poet Celan is preparing himself.
My *Deathfugue*. My black milk of daybreak. Death-master from Germany.
Dein goldenes Haar Marguerite. Dein aschenes Haar Sulamith. Aschenes-Antschel.

Was it sunrise, too, as when Raskolnikov, sleepless, was crossing his bridge?
Perhaps sleepless is why Raskolnikov hates this Jew, this Celan, this Antschel.
If not, maybe he'd love him. Won't he love the prisoners in his camp?

Won't he love and forgive and cherish the poor girl he's been tormenting?
Christian forgiveness all over the place, like brain on your boot.
Though you mustn't forgive, in your plot, Jew on bridge; *Deathfugue* on bridge.

Celan-Antschel goes over the rail. As have many others before him.
There used to be nets down near Boulogne to snare the debris, the bodies,

of prostitutes, bankrupts, sterile young wives, gamblers, and naturally
   Jews.

Celan was so sick of the *Deathfugue* he'd no longer let it be printed.
In the tape of him reading, his voice is songful and fervent, like a cantor's.
When he presented the poem to some artists, they hated the way he
   recited.

His parents had died in the camps. Of typhus the father. Mama probably
   gun.
Celan-Antschel, had escaped. He'd tried to convince them to come, too.
Was that part of it, on the bridge? Was that he wrote in German part, too?

He stood on the bridge over the Seine, looked into the black milk of
   dying,
Jew on bridge, and hauled himself over the rail. *Dein aschenes Haar* . . .
Dostoevsky's Jew, though, is still there. On page something or other.

He must be waiting to see where destiny's plotting will take him. It won't.
He'll just have to wait there forever. Jew on bridge, hanging out of the
   plot.
I try to imagine what he would look like. My father? Grandfathers?
   Greats?

Does he wear black? Would he be like one of those hairy Hasids
where Catherine buys metal for her jewelry, in their black suits and hats,
even in summer, *shvitzing*, in the heat? Crackpots, I think. They depress me.

Do I need forgiveness for my depression? My being depressed like a Jew?
All right then: how Jewish am I? What portion of who I am is a Jew?
I don't want vague definitions, qualifications, here on the bridge of the
   Jew.

I want certainty, *science*: everything you are, do, think; think, do, are,
is precisely twenty-two percent Jewish. Or six-and-a-half. Some nice
   prime.
Your suffering is Jewish. Your resistant, resilient pleasure in living, too,

can be tracked to some Jew on some bridge on page something or other
in some city, some village, some shtetl, some festering *shvitz* of a slum,
with Jews with black hats or not, on their undershirts fringes or not.

Raskolnikov, slouching, shoulders hunched, hands in his pockets,
stinking from all those sleepless nights on his couch, clothes almost
   rotting,
slouching and stinking and shivering and muttering to himself, plods on

past the Jew on the bridge, who's dressed perhaps like anyone else—
coat, hat, scarf, boots—whatever. Our hero would recognize him
by his repulsive, repellent Jew-face daring to hang out in the air.

My father's name also was Paul. As in Celan. His father's name: Benjamin.
As in Walter. Who flung himself from life, too, with vials of morphine.
In some hotel from which he could have reached safety but declined to.

Chose not to. Make it across. Though in fact none of us makes it across.
Aren't we all in that same shitty hotel on that bridge in the shittiest world?
What was he thinking, namesake of my grandpa? Benjamin, Walter,
   knew all.

Past, future, all. He could see perfectly clearly the death he'd miss out on.
You're in a room. Dark. You're naked. Crushed on all sides by others
   naked.
Flesh-knobs. Hairy or smooth. Sweating against you. *Shvitzing* against
   you.

Benjamin would have played it all out in his mind like a fugue. *Deathfugue.*
The sweating, the stinking. And that moment you know you're going to
    die,
and the moment past that, which, if you're Benjamin, Walter, not grandpa,

you know already by heart: the searing through you you realize is your
    grief,
for humans, all humans, their world and their cosmos and oil-cloth stars.
All of it worse than your fear and grief for your own minor death.

So, gulp down the morphine quickly, because of your shame for the
    humans,
what humans can do to each other. Benjamin, grandfather, Walter;
Paul, father, Celan: all the names that ever existed wiped out in shame.

Celan on his bridge. Raskolnikov muttering Dostoevsky under his breath.
Jew on bridge. Raskolnikov-Dostoevsky still in my breath. Under my
    breath.
Black milk of daybreak. *Aschenes Haar.* Antschel-Celan. Ash. Breath.

from

Writers Writing Dying

(2012)

The Day Continues Lovely

With *Fear and Trembling* I studied my Kierkegaard, with *Sickness unto Death*
I contemplated with him my spiritual shortcomings, and it didn't occur to me
until now that in the Kierkegaard I've read he never takes time to actually pray.
Odd . . . This isn't to question his faith—who'd dare?—but his . . . well, agenda.
All those intricate paradoxes of belief he devotes his time to untying, retying.
Can it be that Kierkegaard simply *forgets* to pray, he's so busy untying, retying?
I understand that: I have times I forget to remember I can't pray. *Can't. Pray.*

This June morning just after sparkling daybreak and here I'm not praying.
My three grandsons asleep on their mats on the floor of my study,
shining, all three, more golden than gold, and I'm still not. *Not praying.*
Why aren't I? Even our dog Bwindi sprawled beside Turner, the youngest,
Turner's sleep-curled fist on her back: Why haven't I prayed about them?
I can imagine someday something inside me saying: Well, *why don't you?*
Something inside me. As though suddenly would be *something inside me.*

There's a Buber story I'm probably misrepresenting that touches on this.
A rabbi spends endless hours deciding whether to do good deeds or pray.
He thinks this first, then that: *This might be good; maybe that would be better,*
and suddenly a VOICE that can only be God's erupts: *STOP DAWDLING!*

And *God*, he thinks: he's been chastised by God. *STOP DAWDLING!*
And what happens then? In my anti-Bubering of the tale, everything's lost,
the fool's had his moment with God—even Moses had only how many?—

and he's squandered it because all he could do was stand stunned,
mouth hung metaphorically open, losing his chance to ask for guidance,
but he'd vacillated again and *What happens now?* he wonders in anguish.
Maybe I should get out of this business, find a teaching job, write a book,
on my desolation, my suffering, then he hears again, louder, *STOP! STOP!*
but this time it's his own voice, hopelessly loud, and he knows he'll forever be
in this waiting, this without-God, his glimpse of the Undeniable already waning.

And what about me? Leave aside Kierkegaard, Buber, the rabbis—just me.
Haven't I spent my life trying to make up my mind about *something*?
God, not God; soul, not soul. I'm like the Binary Kid: on, off; off, on.
But isn't that what we all are? Overgrown electrical circuits? Good, bad.
Hate, love. We go crazy trying to gap the space between on and off,
but there is none. Click. Click. Left: Right. Humans kill one another
because there's no room to maneuver inside those minuscule switches.

Meanwhile cosmos roars with so many voices we can't hear ourselves think.
Galaxy on. Galaxy off. Universe on, but another just behind this one,
one more out front waiting for us to be done. They're flowing across us,
sweet swamps of being—and we thrash in them, waving our futile antennae.
. . . Turner's awake now. He smiles, stands; Bwindi yawns and stands, too.

They come to see what I'm doing. Turner leans his head on my shoulder to peek.

What *am* I doing? Thinking of Kierkegaard. Thinking of beauty. Thinking of prayer.

from

All at Once

(2014)

The Last Circus

The horse trainer's horse is a scrawny pony; its ribs show, and when it levers itself onto its battered pedestal, it looks more arthritic than I am. It's trained to nod its head "Yes," but you can tell it wouldn't care if what it's saying is "No," or "Never," or "Leave me alone, please."

His master also plays the clown—when he does, he looks like an accountant down on his luck: he's not very funny, we clap because we want him to be. He also juggles, though he keeps dropping the dumbbells and balls.

The girl who walks the tightrope, three feet off the ground, must be his daughter. Then she's the girl hanging from a long rope her clown-father swings; he lets her plummet down until her face nearly touches the sawdust, then she pops to her feet. Her costume is blotchy, and sags.

Intermission: behind the tent, the most bored lions in the world laze in their fetid cage, refusing to meet our eyes. Then a clutch of battered trailers, clotheslines slung from them out to some trees: T-shirts, towels, underclothes worn all but to air. Scattered beneath are crumpled pizza boxes, plastic bags, beer bottles, cans, other indecipherable junk.

The show begins again, the sparse audience climbs back onto the bleachers. One man sits engulfed by his children: a sleeping two-year-old sprawls across his lap, her head lolling on his shoulder; he kicks her gooey, half-eaten, half-melted glop of cotton candy into the void beneath; a larger child, another girl, sits on one of his knees, wriggling with delight, her circus banner waving in his face; and the last, a baby in the crook of his arm, he manages with the same hand that holds it to offer it some cola in a cup. A little dribbles on the baby's chin, and with a corner of his shirt he wipes it up, pats the disconsolate infant in his lap, who's just woken crying, and then, when the clown appears again, he cheers, stamps, whistles, and, like Shiva, foliates another pair of hands and heartily applauds.

Again

One of my grandsons is running through the park towards me to show me something he's found—a long white feather—I can see it from here—probably from one of the herons that come at dawn to fish in the pond.

It doesn't matter which grandson it is: in my memory, it could be one, or another, or all—I'd prefer it were all, each in his brilliant singularity, each in his union with the rest.

There's a broad plane tree between us, and for some reason my grandson as he runs keeps moving left and then right, so he disappears behind the trunk of the tree, appears again, disappears, appears, vivid in the brilliant sunlight, again is gone, again is there, all the while beaming with pride at bearing such treasure to share with me.

Also he calls my name each time he appears, and as I stand waiting, listening, watching him materialize again, it comes to me that if that old legend of having your life flash before you as you die is true, I'll have this all again, and again.

Silence

The heron methodically pacing like an old-time librarian down the stream through the patch of woods at the end of the field, those great wings tucked in as neatly as clean sheets, is so intent on keeping her silence, extracting one leg, bending it like a paper clip, placing it back, then bending the other, the first again, that her concentration radiates out into the listening world, and everything obediently hushes, the ragged grasses that rise from the water, the light-sliced vault of sparkling aspens.

Then abruptly a flurry, a flapping, her lifting from the gravitied earth, her swoop out over the field, her banking and settling on a lightning-stricken oak, such a gangly, unwieldy contraption up there in the barkless branches, like a still Adam's-appled adolescent; then the cry, cranky, coarse, and wouldn't the waiting world laugh aloud if it could with glee?

The Broom

The wide-bristled brooms that late at night in bus stations glide noiselessly over the terrazzo floors, as though they'd achieved the most intimate, unintimidated relation to duration, to time; as though, despite the tired salesman half asleep on a bench, the two college-kid lovers impatiently waiting in the dark sanctity of a Greyhound for the bus to depart so they can continue their furtive petting, the group of Asian women who huddle around a pay phone, listening, listening, waiting, hanging up then dialing again an instant later (what betrayal might they be involved in, what abandonment, desertion?), and the semi-winos and the semi-paranoid who are allowed to slump and sleep in these sanctuaries reserved for them, as well as we who are blessèd by the scriptures of our tickets—as though all of this might be systematically transcended, lifted from the precincts of a mere motorless implement patterning methodically over trivial shining expanses with a mad geometrical exactness, to a process more comprehensive, a tractor, say, in a wheat field after harvest, when every centimeter must be disked and harrowed, and all beneath a brutal August sun none of us trapped here has beheld for centuries, only fancied, dreamed of, here in this hallowed, middle place of bland fluorescent longing.

from
Catherine's Laughter

Talk

Catherine and I, for some long-forgotten reason, have both been irritable all day, touchy, preoccupied, moody, and gloomy. Dinner is peaceful, though, and when we finish Catherine asks, "Are we going to make love tonight?"

I answer, "If I'm talking to you."

"You don't have to talk," Catherine says.

Oaks

After dinner, still at the table, I'm writing in my little notebook, scribbling fast, when Catherine says she'd like to take a walk. When I tell her I'm busy she takes the empty dishes into the kitchen, then comes back.

"Come on, take a walk."

"I'm writing," I tell her.

"Take your notebook. You can take your wine, too."

"Wait just a minute," I say.

"You need a bigger notebook," Catherine says then. "I'll buy you a bigger notebook."

"I don't need a bigger notebook, and don't get me one."

"That's why I said it," Catherine says. "I just wanted to hear you say that. Let's go for a walk."

Finally I give up, give in, we stroll out across the park near our house and come to the pair of gigantic old oaks Catherine particularly loves. The trunk of each tree is about five feet across, and they stand close together, leaning a little as though making room for each other.

They're in full-leaved gorgeousness right now, and when we get to them Catherine says, "You have to come in here," and leads me between them.

"Now close your eyes," she says.

"Why?"

"Because there are all those branches above us," she answers, "and beneath us the roots. You have to listen."

I listen. "But I don't . . ." I start to object.

"You have to come stand here every day, then you will," Catherine answers, not laughing now. "You'll see, you will."

from

Selected Later Poems

(2015)

The World and Hokusai

Like a little boy with his daddy world takes Hokusai's hand to be led
    through the wilds of doubt
and derision yes even derision because so many crybabies keep yowling
    Stop, World! You hurt!
but Hokusai with all his bequeathments keeps on and poor put-upon
    world sighs with relief

because here's Hokusai's elephant thirty feet tall with tiny bald either
    elf-creatures or angels
or maybe who knows even regular humans in striped pants and smocks
    trying to scale it
to figure out what it could possibly be but isn't it clear that Hokusai's
    elephant has to be *world?*

Look how it winks from the side of its wise patient eye and the shelves of
    skin hanging across it!
No actual elephant ever had so many Fuji wrinkles and cracks—it has to
    be Hokusai's world
and who else could cook up an elephant-world but him? The rest of us
    find just living so hard

we have to convince ourselves not to give it all up, and do what? . . . Take
    naps? Write a book?
Anyway here's Hokusai!—yay!—pen sharp as a dart and Look he pro-
    claims I've drawn a soldier
firing a crazy cannon who knows why into some waves The smoke! The
    turmoil! The tumult!

But note also please how the soldier is smiling looking just fine indif-
    ferent unconcerned bland

and old Hokusai must have been smiling too into his fist elephants
    cannons really after all
what excruciations could afflict someone who'd sign work "Seen with the
    eyes of a blind man"?

But what if he ever gets tired of dragging petulant world behind him
    what if he closes up shop
who'd keep it going? Not me I'm just an old word-spider slung here
    scritch-scratching the keys—
Hokusai would be laughing but where would I find an elephant where
    would I come up with a world?

Beethoven Invents the Species Again

for Richard Goode

1.

As is the case every day though we don't always know it here we are
    waiting for Beethoven

to kick-start the species again get us going on being wholly human again
    we're anxious about it

as usual existence as usual driving us to distraction we muttering
    hatchlings fragmented

just as we were when we were half-beings before music found us it took
    so long for music to find us

remember? back when we'd taught ourselves only to chip carve hammer
    spear points or blades

while our psyches stricken with longing kept burbling up blurred
    intimations of *more* we mixtures

condemned to inhabit recalcitrant realms where tree was tree hill hill
    earth soil lake etcetera

all *thing*-things entrenched in stony obstinate factness though we kept
    wanting more than fact

more even than what we could brain-glue together centaur minotaur
    harpy please more more

we cried always in pieces hoping for what we still couldn't speak as again
    we hoisted our hatchets

but wait someone said wait Beethoven still says says again always what
    of sound world-sound or wind

wolf-sound or water might the way be in listening rather than making or
    thinking even or praying?

2.

Not only Beethoven still says Mozart also and Bach and Schubert
    Chopin Ella and Woody and Miles
and the rest we can trace all of them back because somewhere in us we
    still hear that first hollow pipe
in a cave then Hermes devising the lyre and Orpheus tuning it up and
    before you know it harp fiddle

and piano! bravo! finally Beethoven's piano listen again how the notes
    knit together then the chords
how the melodies climb the beckoning rows of their scales and we're
    lifted once more to coherence
we and that ravenous void in us brought together for this shining time as
    music again fashions

the hallowed place where our doubts and frailties are lathed like dross
    from our ancient confusions
and where as we attend we're no longer half-things we once-collages we're
    whole who couldn't tell
if we were hawks humans horses we're complete now not hanging out of
    the scabbard of matter

but caught by contained and spun from the music that embodies those
    ever unlikely connections
while in our rapture at being transformed again into musical selves a note
    a chord at a time we exist
as we knew all along thank you Beethoven thank you the rest we should
    have and now once again do

from

Falling Ill

(2017)

Box

Volume I once believed of adhesive fragments
over which I presumed I'd always preside
but I'm informed has filled with renegade

somethings replacing the bits over which
I now assert nothing rather I'm more
a box in which amass insidious devourers

and when I picture myself I'm mostly
transparent not in the accusing greys of an x-ray
but in a substance something like what

was once called *spirit* imperceptible yet insistent
is it surprising then to imagine I might want
to flee from this box that heaves and groans

like a tree blasted by wind the cries of innocent
root twig and branch coursing through
this absence within me but no longer mine?

First Dying

He thought he knew dying the near edge
of dying because everything was so taxing
every moment more taxing because waking

was taxing because rising from his chair
too taxing so it seemed reasonable to sprawl
on the reliable chair and because he was this tired

he thought he must know the onset of dying
the lurch into dying the first task of dying
did he think this had something to do with dying

believing his duty now was surrender
did he dare think dying was submission
to conditions not wholly unfamiliar dying might

be not even unpleasant he'd think even
lifting yourself on your flimsy legs to be blown
about in blind time like a guttering flame

You

Always beside me always so closely to me
that you might be within me or be me
especially that night I couldn't breathe

then you were emphatically with me
I saw you there not gasping with
me as I gasped but radiant with hope

though hope's such an insignificant
term compared to the panic barely suppressed
I couldn't help seeing in your eyes

as you waited and I couldn't help either
not allowing death to enter the drama
because that might undo you and I needed

you even just from that side of my life
even defined by your valiant hope and
being your self in a way I'd never before known

Eyes

When I close my eyes or I should say when
my eyes close because I don't will them to close
they decide despite me and they close

and to open them have them working again
I have to come up with a *reason* unlike when
they clicked and flew open as soon as they shut

unless I'd closed them for sleep or love or to keep
myself from being afraid while now being
behind my closed lids is more than seductive

it's normal and along with it the temptation keeps
taking me why not stay why not let myself stay
here so that other unspeakable thought-thing I dare

not confront might not take me and how not believe
if I were to stay here behind this veil the appalling
truth wouldn't when it arrived surprise me at all

Secrets

If I keep secret from you that I'm spinning
if I don't hint to you I feel I'm falling
if I keep hidden from you that I'm fainting

the next death-thing wants on its own
to say I'm expiring or on the way to expiring
not expiring in itself but in some strange way

close to or even adjacent to it but there's no
reason that sharing with you the spinning
should evoke a premonition of expiring

still certain I am I'm far from any kind
of extinction can you hear that can you
and I hear that waking together in which

I'm not "spinning" my head not "turning"
I'm only waiting as everything must for its
long-concealed turnings to be revealed

Impatience

Get it over with's not what Adam would
have shouted to serpent when his going began
not get me out of here get me over with

never is more likely what he'd have groaned
unlike that chip of me that petrifies
not daring to postulate any sort of departure

but keeps anyway telling itself over and over
not like begging to oh I don't know pick
your king your old god get this over with

you would say pull up this halfway death
finish this endless non-suffering suffering
release me though I don't really mean it

for wouldn't I have to tear myself to leave
my beloved and wouldn't my beloved be torn
too and isn't it intolerable to entertain that?

Friends

Those of you who've gone before how precious
you remain how little your essential nature
has altered and insofar as it has I can't grasp

how you might be other than you ever were
surely you aren't wholly "gone" though that's
undeniably your essence now to have gone

surely you haven't even metaphorically risen
or descended it's just that you're not *available*
to those left behind unavailable for what

except the generation of future memories
I don't know that's the painful aspect of love
gone to no longer generate memories to share

here we laughed here danced all falls away
only the tattered snatches of what we call past
echo out from the isolate provinces of time

Embrace

This once I don't know and can't guess
why it should be this once when we come
together bring our bodies together

your arms round my neck my arms
round your waist this once there's a poignancy
to our embrace this once there's a kind

of not desperation but force a force
that takes us both and presses us against
each other more than "presses" hurls us

each to and against the other in a way we've
never experienced before and I can't tell if
it represents or embodies a recognition

of mortality a premonition of what will be
coming to take us or whether this is beyond
us beyond what's coming to us beyond all

Lonely

How strange to be lonely one day and not
the next when I remember so clearly
how the passion not to be lonely was the enduring

need of my first life the illusion that being
alone would injure me wound me neutralize me
leave me with no actual ego I could believe in

then how long after would it have been came
the realization that the most acute moments
of solitude were in the company of others

it didn't matter loved ones or not only a few
a frightening few you most of all brought
respite and this is surely redundant presence

a presence that effused around us joining us
bringing us closer touching or not so now
the thought of leaving you alone tears so

Air

Not air as on that island the weeks of love's onset
not air even on those mornings with mild
waves insinuating themselves on the shore

we looked out on nor the cypress intensifying
the scent of the breezes nor the breezes themselves
but a medium rather of hidden arcane qualities

such was the air in the first days of illness
enfolding me in a texture I'd never known
as though in another genre of simple being

something I'd not merely bring into my lungs
but capture and devour so pure was it
so definitive as it churned so powerfully

through me so I'd wonder if the part of me
that was me knew already how precious air
soon would become and remain glorious air

Index of Titles and
First Lines

A basset hound with balls, 197

A dense, low, irregular overcast is flowing
rapidly in over the city from the middle
South, 82

A dream of method first, in which mind is
malleable, its products as revisable as
sentences, 97

After Auschwitz, 149

After dinner, still at the table, I'm writing
in my little notebook, scribbling, 224

After this much time, it's still impossible.
The SS man with his stiff hair and his
uniform, 20

Again, 218

Again and again. Again lips, again
breast, again hand, thigh, loin and
bed and bed, 25

A garden I usually never would visit;
oaks, roses, the scent of roses I usually
wouldn't remark, 132

Air, 242

All but Always, 199

Almost as good as her passion, I'll think,
almost as good as her presence, her
physical grace, 137

Although he's apparently the youngest
(his little Rasta-beard is barely down and
feathers), xv, 131

Although I'm apparently alone, with a
pleasant but unextraordinary feeling of
self-sufficiency, 103

Always beside me always so closely to me,
235

Always in the dream I seemed conscious
of myself having the dream even as I
dreamed it, 125

Alzheimer's: The Husband, 77

Alzheimer's: The Wife, 76

A middle-aged woman, quite plain, to be
polite about it, and somewhat stout, to
be more courteous still, 160

An insistence in dream on a succession
of seemingly urgent but possibly
purposeless tasks, 105

As a child, in the half-dark, as you wait on
the edge of her bed for her to sleep, 140

As I'm reading Tsvetaeva's essays, 188

As is the case every day though we don't
always know it here we are waiting for
Beethoven, 229

As soon as the old man knew he was
actually dying, even before anyone else
would admit it, 93

A summer cold. No rash. No fever. Nothing.
But a dozen times during the night I
wake, 23

A whole section of the city I live in has been urban renewed, some of it torn down, 17

Back, 201
Bed, The, 135
Beds squalling, squealing, muffled in hush; beds pitching, leaping, immobile as mountains, 135
Beethoven Invents the Species Again, 229
Being Alone, 9
Blocks of time fall upon me, adhere for a moment, then move astonishingly away, fleeting, dissolving, 101
Box, 233
Bread, 17
Broom, The, 220

Cassandra, Iraq, 190
Catherine and I, for some long-forgotten reason, have both been irritable all, 223
Charge, The, 105
Chop, hack, slash; chop, hack, slash; cleaver, boning knife, ax—, 192
City in the Hills, The, 80
Coffin Store, The, 193
Combat, 41
Covenant, The, 123
Crime, The, 107

Dance, The, 160
Dawn, 72
Day Continues Lovely, The, 211
Day for Anne Frank, A, xiii, 3
Deciphering and encoding, to translate, fabricate, revise; the abstract star, the real star, 117
Deep asleep, perfect immobility, no apparent evidence of consciousness or of dream, 61
Depths, 157
Doe, The, 169
Dress, The, 152

Embrace, 240
Even So, 78
Exterior: Day, 139
Eyes, 236

Fear, The, 119
First Desires, 85
First Dying, 234
First I did my thing, that's to say her thing, to her, for her, 201
Foundation, The, 202
Friends, 239
From My Window, 53

Gaffe, The, 185
Gap, The, 115
Garden (Symbols), 132
Gas Station, The, 64
Get it over with's not what Adam would, 238
Grace, 137

He'd been a clod, he knew, yes, always aiming toward his vision of the good life, always acting on it, 77
He hasn't taken his eyes off you since we walked in, although you seem not to notice particularly, 89
He's not sure how to get the jack on—he must have recently bought the car, although it's an ancient, 73
He thought he knew dying the near edge, 234
History, 113
Hog Heaven, 36
Hooks, xiv, 69
How strange to be lonely one day and not, 241

Ice, 147
I'd like every girl in the world to have a poem of her own, 13

If I keep secret from you that I'm spinning, 237

If that someone who's me yet not me yet who judges me is always with me, 185

If you were to possess a complicated, 199

I have escaped in the dream; I was in danger, at peril, at immediate, furious, frightening risk, 113

I look onto an alley here, 3

I'm on a parapet looking down, 157

Impatience, 238

In my dream of unspecific anxiety, nothing is what it should be, nothing acts as it should, 119

In my unlikeliest dream, my dead are with me again, companions again, in an ordinary way, 123

Instinct, xv, 131

In the dream of death where I listen, the voices of the dream keep diminishing, fading away, 121

In those days, those days which exist for me only as the most elusive memory now, 152

Invisible Mending, 165

It stinks. It stinks and it stinks and it stinks and it stinks, 36

It was like listening to the record of a symphony before you knew anything at all about the music, 85

I've been trying for hours to figure out who I was reminded of by the welterweight fighter, 41

I wanted to take up room. What a strange dream! I wanted to take up as much room as I could, 111

I was lugging my death from Kampala to Kraków, 193

I was walking home down a hill near our house on a balmy afternoon under the blossoms, 170

Jew on Bridge, 204

Knot, The, 117

Last Circus, The, 217

Late afternoon and difficult to tell if those are mountains, soft with mist, off across the lake, 80

Lens, The, 71

Light, 125

Like a little boy with his daddy world takes Hokusai's hand to be led through the wilds of doubt, 227

Lonely, 241

Love: Beginnings, 83

Lover, The, 143

Marina, 188

Maybe she missed the wife, or the wife's better dinner parties, but she never forgave him, 143

Method, The, 97

My Fly, 129

My Mother's Lips, 56

Near dusk, near a path, near a brook, 169

Near the Haunted Castle, 34

Never on one single pore Eternity, 9

Not air as on that island the weeks of love's onset, 242

Oaks, 224

Of Childhood the Dark, 174

Often I have thought that after my death, not in death's void as we usually think it, 133

Often in our garden these summer evenings a thrush, 195

One more thing to keep, 172

One of my grandsons is running through the park towards me to show, 218

One of those great, garishly emerald flies that always look freshly generated from fresh excrement, 129

One vast segment of the tree, the very topmost, bows ceremoniously against a breath of breeze, 159

On Learning of a Friend's Illness, 58
Owen: Seven Days, 162

Peace, 70
Petit Salvié, Le, 84
Politics, 91
Possibly because she's already so striking—
    tall, well-dressed, very clear, pure
    skin—, xiv, 69
Prodigy, The, 79

Raskolnikov hasn't slept. For days.
    In his brain, something like white,
    204
Reading: The Gym, 74
Reading: Winter, 73
Realms, 133
Room, 111
Rush Hour, 81

Secrets, 237
Shade, The, 23
Shadows, 99
She answers the bothersome telephone,
    takes the message, forgets the message,
    forgets who called, 76
Shells, 109
Shells of fearful insensitivity that I keep
    having to disadhere from my heart, how
    dream you?, 109
She's magnificent, as we imagine women
    must be, 190
Silence, 219
Silence, The, 89
Singing, The, 170
Snapshots of her grandchildren and great-
    grandchildren are scattered on the old
    woman's lap, 71
Solid, The, 103
Someone has folded a coat under the
    boy's head, someone else, an Arab
    businessman in not very good
    French, 81

So often and with such cruel fascination I
    have dreamed the implacable void that
    contains dream, 115
So quickly, and so slowly . . . In the tiny
    elevator of the flat you'd borrowed on the
    Rue de Pondicherry, 84
Spit, 20
Splendid that I'd revel even more in the
    butterflies harvesting pollen, 182
Spring: the first morning when that one true
    block of sweet, laminar, complex scent
    arrives, 53
Stalled an hour beside a row of abandoned,
    graffiti-stricken factories, 156
Storm, The, 82
Such longing, such urging, such warmth
    towards, such force towards, so much
    ardor and desire, 120
Sully: Sixteen Months, 172
Swifts, 161

Talk, 223
Tar, 50
That astonishing thing that happens when
    you crack a needle-awl into a block of
    ice, 147
The bench he's lying on isn't nearly wide
    enough for the hefty bulk of his torso
    and shoulders, 74
The first morning of mist after days of
    draining, unwavering heat along the
    shore: a breath, 72
The first morning of Three Mile Island:
    those first disquieting, uncertain,
    mystifying hours, 50
The heron methodically pacing like an old-
    time librarian down the stream, 219
The horse trainer's horse is a scrawny pony;
    its ribs show, and when it levers, 217
The morning is so gray that the grass is
    gray and the side of the white horse
    grazing, 58
The way, playing an instrument, when you
    botch a passage you have to stop before
    you can go on again—, 75

The wide-bristled brooms that late at night
in bus stations glide noiselessly, 220
They drift unobtrusively into the dream,
they linger, then they depart, but they
emanate, always, 99
They're at that stage where so much desire
streams between them, so much frank
need and want, 83
They're discussing the political situation
they've been watching evolve in a faraway
country, 91
This is a story. You don't have to think about
it, it's make-believe, 34
This is before I'd read Nietzsche. Before
Kant or Kierkegaard, even before
Whitman and Yeats, 64
This once I don't know and can't guess, 240
Those of you who've gone before how
precious, 239
Though no shyer than the others—while her
pitch is being checked she beams out at
the audience, 79
Though she's seventy-four, has three
children, five grown grandchildren (one
already pregnant), 78
Three women old as angels, 165
Thrush, 195
Time: 1972, 140
Time: 1978, 141
To Listen, 121
Train, The, 156
Tree, 159
Two actors are awkwardly muscling a coffin
out of a doorway draped in black funeral
hangings, 139

Uncanny to realize one was *here*, so much, 174
Until I asked her to please stop doing it and
was astonished to find that she not only
could, 56

Vehicle: Forgetting, 75
Violence in the dream, violation of body
and spirit; torment, mutilation, butchery,
debasement, 107
Vocations, 101
Volume I once believed of adhesive
fragments, 233

Wait, 192
Waking Jed, 61
Watch me, I'm running, watch me, I'm
dancing, I'm air, 202
We, 197
We'd wanted to make France,
149
We fight for hours, through dinner,
through the endless evening,
who, 70
Well here I, 162
What could be more endearing, on a long,
too quiet, lonely evening in an unfamiliar
house, 141
When, 93
When I close my eyes or I should say when,
236
Why this much fascination with you, little
loves, why this what feels like, oh, hearts,
161
With *Fear and Trembling* I studied my
Kierkegaard, with *Sickness unto Death*,
211
With *Ignorance*, 25
World, The, 182
World and Hokusai, The, 227

You (from *A Dream of Mind*),
120
You (from *Falling Ill*), 235
Yours, 13